WHISPERS
from
HEAVEN

WHISPERS
from
HEAVEN

Partnering with God
in Powerful Prayer
and Effective Intercession

BENI JOHNSON

DESTINY IMAGE® PUBLISHERS, INC.
P.O. Box 310, Shippensburg, PA 17257-0310
"Promoting Inspired Lives."

This book and all other Destiny Image and Destiny Image Fiction
books are available at Christian bookstores and distributors
worldwide.

For more information on foreign distributors,
call 717-532-3040.

Reach us on the Internet: www.destinyimage.com.

ISBN 13 TP: 978-0-7684-6469-6

ISBN 13 eBook: 978-0-7684-6206-7

ISBN 13 HC: 978-0-7684-6205-0

For Worldwide Distribution, Printed in the U.S.A.

1 2 3 4 5 6 7 8 / 27 26 25 24 23

CONTENTS

INTRODUCTION

By Bill Johnson

I have had a front-row seat to the adventure of a lifetime: the transformation of one who loved and served God into one who became a true friend of God. My wife of 49 years, Beni Johnson, was that person. She wrote and taught from a place of love and tenderness to the Holy Spirit that made others yearn for such a relationship. The most beautiful fruit of her example and teaching has been to see others enter into that same deep place with God. It was possible for others to enter as it wasn't complicated at all. It only required surrender. Absolute surrender.

I remember the day someone spoke to my wife, in the middle of his sermon, and told her she was called to intercession—but that she would find the secret to blending intercession with joy. That word did not make her happy. Every intercessor she knew was depressed. I'm so happy she didn't want to be like that. We were raising three children and didn't need that kind of negative influence in our home. What happened in the following months and years was nothing short of miraculous. This one who wanted nothing to do with that kind of ministry found a place in the heart of God where she could maintain her assignment to pray, and pray deeply, without losing her joy for Him and for life itself. Her breakthrough has become a template for many.

Without question, the day we live in is quite serious. The destiny of nations lies in the balance. But Beni illustrates through her writing how to live in that place of personal victory and joy, regardless of the surrounding circumstances.

Whispers from Heaven is an invitation. It's an invitation to tenderness, to friendship, to personal transformation. I pray that you respond to this opportunity with a resounding *yes*. And then put on your seatbelt, as God will take you into an adventure that will shape the rest of your days. The nations ache for your *yes*.

— Bill Johnson
Author of *The Way of Life* and *Open Heavens*
Senior Leader of Bethel Church, Redding, CA

JOY AND INTERCESSION

I grew up in a church where the "intercessors" did not look like happy people a lot of the time. From my small perspective, all those who were intercessors were the ones who walked around with what looked to me like very heavy burdens. The intercessors always looked sad to me, and I don't remember seeing them smile. As I got older, I remember thinking, "I do not want to be an intercessor." I didn't know it was possible for intercessors to be happy. I had a lot to learn.

For many years, I didn't know I was an intercessor. When I look back now, I can see all the signs: I spent so much time carrying so many feelings inside of me and internalizing them as if they were my own. For example, I would often walk into a room filled with people and start feeling and hearing their thoughts—thoughts which were often very negative. Not realizing that all of those feelings that I was experiencing were the gift that the Bible calls "discernment of spirits," I would carry those burdensome emotions as my own instead of releasing them in prayer. As a result, I became depressed. I became a "quiet one."

When I turned 16, I had an encounter with God that changed my life. After that encounter, I didn't do anything unless I prayed about it. I would go to my closet and open it and ask Jesus what I should wear that day. But I still did not understand my gifting and how to pray. Even though I was going through this amazing time with God in part of my life, I was not releasing to Him all of the things that I was feeling and picking up around me. I continued to internalize. I had no one to tell me that the emotions I was feeling inside of me and sensing around me were things that I needed to be praying about.

I met Bill at Bethel Church in 1969, when his father was the pastor of the church. We met during the Jesus Movement, got married, and spent five years on staff at Bethel before we moved to Weaverville, California, to pastor a small church in the mountains. I had a prayer life, but it was just a general prayer life. I prayed for my kids and my family or things that were going on in the church. I prayed because I thought that was what I was supposed to do. I didn't pray out of relationship with the Holy Spirit.

In 1995, renewal came to our church in Weaverville. It was a time of great refreshing and joy. It was also a time when the Holy Spirit stirred up my heart, releasing me to be who I am. A brand-new season was coming. In this time of stirring, I felt Him speak to me a word that would change my life. I heard these words: "I want you to carry joy and intercession." My first thought was, "Is that possible?"

I know that there are so many aspects of the Kingdom I've unintentionally put into human-sized boxes. God, help me to break free of the limits of my own understanding so I can truly see from Your perspective. Show me any areas where I've limited Your love, peace, or joy. Dismantle any religious or political structures I've created around my idea of You. I want to know the truth!

BIRTHING IDENTITY

When renewal hit, people were experiencing so much freedom. I had two different experiences during that time that I would call life-changing encounters with God. One of those experiences happened in Toronto, at John and Carol Arnott's church, Toronto Airport Christian Fellowship (TACF). My parents, my husband, and I were attending a conference there on the Father's Blessing, which was the pulse of the whole outpouring there at TACF.

After one of the meetings, Bill and I got up to go and walked to the back of the room where there were people everywhere on the floor, much laughter, and Holy Spirit drunkenness. Acts 2:15 (NKJV) says, *"For these are not drunk, as you suppose, since it is only the third hour of the day."* When the Holy Spirit's power hit the disciples in the upper room, they looked and acted like they were drunk.

Have you ever noticed that drunken people don't care what other people think about what they are doing at that moment? Well, there was such a man at that meeting that night. We noticed him staggering around the back, laying his hands on people. As he did, they would fall to the ground. God was using that man as a Holy Spirit conduit. Some would laugh with Holy Spirit laughter; others would shake under the power of the Holy Spirit. I looked over at him, and we made eye contact, and he headed my way. I had my arm in Bill's arm, but when the man got over to me, he reached out with one finger and touched my arm. I immediately fell to the ground and began shaking violently. Bill had to let go of my arm.

For 20 minutes or so, I shook so hard. At one point, a woman came over to me and asked if I was in good shape. I told her I was, and she just said, "Then, more Lord." And off I went again. It finally subsided a little so that I could get up. But I needed help back to the room.

The next day, we went back to the morning session. As the speaker began speaking something about the Father's love, I felt the presence of God and began to cry. I asked the Lord what had gone on the night before. "What was that all about?" I heard these words: "I was shaking out of you the strongholds of your life and birthing who you are." From that day on, the fear that had guided my life left. The stronghold had been broken. I became a different person through that unusual encounter with God.

I open myself up, Lord, to a life-changing encounter with You. I want Your presence to invade, to shake off anything that I'm carrying that is not of You. Reveal to me any areas of my personality that do not align with Your design for me. Have Your way in me, God. I give up my right to understand, control, or maintain my dignity before others. I want You, whatever the cost.

A NEW DAY

When we have life-changing encounters with the Lord, the devil doesn't just sit back and say, "Oh, I can't tempt her anymore." No, he tries to come and get us to make agreement with him. The devil wants us to agree with our old lifestyle patterns.

Once we agree with him, he has control again. The devil will allow a familiar spirit to come to us and get us to go back to thinking old ways, but now we are equipped with a supernatural strength to say, "No."

So when a familiar spirit, such as self-pity, comes and tries to get us to agree and say, "Yes, that's the way I am," we can now say (because the stronghold has been removed), "No, that is not who I am anymore." I felt as though God had given me a power tool for my life and the strength to use it against the lies from the devil.

Right after my encounter experience in Toronto, I had another life-changing experience. I was at a women's retreat in Mt. Shasta, California. I remember sitting in the back of the room during the worship. I was minding my own business, and Holy Spirit showed up, and I began to cry, the kind of crying that comes from way down deep inside of you. A friend came over to me and asked if I was OK and if I knew what was happening to me. All I knew was that this was God, that something was happening to me, and that it was very deep. I couldn't stop crying. I began to feel like something was being pulled out of me and that something was being activated in me.

After that night, everything began to change. I actually felt like a new person, like my personality had gone through a change. Boldness had come over me. I found that, for the next several months, all I could do was cry. It wasn't a sad cry but a cry that came from a new love that I had found. Every time I would think about God and His goodness or someone would talk about what God was doing or even mention the name of Jesus, I would begin crying. I was falling in love with the Holy Spirit.

Thank You, Holy Spirit, that You never leave me on my own. Thank You that I can trust You not only to lead me into moments of powerful transformation, but also to stay close to me as I walk out my freedom daily. You know me, You see me, You are for me. Give me eyes to see anything that tries to come against Your plan for my life.

HOLY GHOST PARTY

Because the renewal brought refreshing and the Father's heart was being poured out, I found myself, like so many others, lost in His amazing presence. I would go into a deep place of intimacy with Him. I had never experienced anything like that in my whole life of being a believer. I'd been raised in the church, and loving God was all that I knew. But this was different. At first it scared me because it was so deep and very intense. I didn't know if this was right. Nobody had told me about this. What was it?

Before I experienced this new level of freedom with the Lord, leading groups and Bible studies had been torture. But this all began to change. I began to see myself as a completely different person. I began to see myself as no longer shy and no longer introverted. I did not care what people thought about me anymore. I remember that, all of a sudden, it became really easy to get up and share Jesus and to share testimonies and to talk about what God was doing. I no longer felt torture related to getting up and talking in front of people; there was such a freedom. I, along with those in the Bible studies and groups I was leading, felt like we were in the midst of a Holy Ghost party. Everyone was getting set free and getting full of joy.

At this point, my prayer life really began to change. My prayer life was not so much about asking for things anymore but just about wanting to be with the Lord. And I would just worship Him for an hour or more at a time. Music has played a vital part in the personal renewal of my life. I am able to tap into His presence through the tool of worship music. I would put a worship CD on, sit in God's presence, and enjoy Him. His presence was deep inside of me, in my spirit man.

This happened for a year in Weaverville, and then we moved to Redding to pastor at Bethel. In this whole process of renewal, I was enjoying the presence of God. I was enjoying Him and Him alone. In this process, I began experiencing something unusual. I began seeing pictures of people's faces. I would see cities and towns. I would see situations and problems, and I would find myself, out of that place of intimacy, crying out to God for resolution in the things that I was seeing. I remember one time, after God showed me something, saying, "Oh God, that is such a good idea. Go do that there; take care of that there." It was such a new experience—being able to tap into that deep place of God. I did not realize at the time that I was experiencing true intercession—how it is supposed to be. To be honest, I kind of fell into it.

Lord, I want to experience an even greater depth of intimacy with You. I give You my time, my schedule, even my desire to get things done. You are my priority, my greatest treasure. I value Your presence above all else. Lead me into the secret place with You. I want to know Your heart.

THE HEARTBEAT OF HEAVEN

hen renewal hit our church, everything began to change. So many people were being ushered into His presence during that season. So many, at that time, were caught up into Heaven, into that completeness. We began to hear the heartbeat of Heaven. This depth of His presence was new for many. What we learned was that we were moving into true intercession.

There was a mixture of love, joy, and extreme heartbreak. This heartbreak that we would feel was from the extreme, intense love that our Father has for His children all over the world. Like in the story of the prodigal son, we felt the Father missing His children and longing for them to come back to Him and His love. And we found that when we would let ourselves experience the longing of a Heavenly Father who was desperate to pour His love upon us, we could almost become "addicted" to His glorious presence. We found that, once we experienced that depth of His love, we desired nothing on Earth more than to be in the presence of our Heavenly Father.

In such times, I often *see* faces, places, and situations in my mind's eye. I often feel as if God is showing me things that I need to think about and *brood over* in the way that a mother hen broods over her eggs. Genesis 1:1 says, *"Earth was a soup of nothingness, a bottomless emptiness, an inky blackness. God's Spirit brooded like a bird above the watery abyss"* (MSG). To be honest, most of the time when I am in this place, I just agree. I agree with the plans that God already has for people's lives, for regions, and for the earth. "Yes God, do that God…go there, Father…that's amazing, Lord Jesus." When I pray this way, I feel as though I am praying from His heart and calling into existence the very desires that are already in the heart of God.

In those times, I feel as though I become the very womb of God. *"He who believes in Me, as the Scripture said, 'From his innermost being will flow rivers of living water'"* (John 7:38 NASB). The words *innermost being* come from the word *koilia*, which means "womb." We are the womb of God. In our intercessions, we are creating and birthing the things of Heaven. We carry the life of the Kingdom within us (see Luke 17:21). It will flow out of us in our intercessions.

Thank You, Father, that You long to pour Your love out on the world. Give me eyes to see and ears to hear Your heartbeat for this moment in time. Break my heart open so that I might experience Your heart for world. Help me to align myself with Your presence so that I might agree with what You are doing in the world.

LEAVE AGENDAS
AT THE DOOR

When we go into God's presence and tap into the realm of Heaven, we position ourselves to receive great breakthrough. One of the things that we need to be careful about is going before God with our own agendas. Sometimes I think we go before God and already have an idea of what we want God to do. In doing so, we close ourselves off from receiving from and partnering with God and what He may want to do in the moment. In fact, God may want to do something completely different. It is almost as if we say, "Here, God, here is my idea; now do it my way." When we do that, we handcuff God. We are no longer partnering with Him.

Often, when people ask me to pray for them, they come with an agenda—or an idea—of what they want to ask God to do. When I am praying for people and I ask them what they need prayer for, sometimes their requests are not what is on God's agenda for the moment. We need to learn how to be sensitive and move with the Holy Spirit. We need to listen to the heartbeat of God and not always present our ideas to Him. It's not about whether agendas are wrong or right, but when I just want to spend time with God and feel His presence, I don't bring any agenda.

God, so often I come to You with my own agenda during prayer. Forgive me for allowing my worries and needs to overshadow all that You long to show me. I lay down my attempt at control. I give up my timeline. Show me what You want to do in this moment. You know the things that are on my heart; now help me to hear all that is on Yours.

PARTNERING WITH US

Intercession is just the fruit of being with Him. It is birthed in my own heart simply by spending time with Him. I go into His presence to love Him, to experience "Spirit to spirit"—His Spirit with my spirit. When I experienced this for the first time, I remember just being with Him and feeling our hearts connecting. It felt like my heart was picking up the same heartbeat as His—pouring upon me "liquid love" from His heart. His heart was broken for humanity. Our two hearts are intertwined. When you feel that, when you see His heart broken and His amazing love, your only response can be to pray with burning passion—with compassion for a lost generation.

> *Whatever God has promised gets stamped with the Yes of Jesus. In him, this is what we preach and pray, the great Amen, God's Yes and our Yes together, gloriously evident* (2 Corinthians 1:20 MSG).

The amazing thing to me is that God is waiting for us to enter into Him. He is longing for us to see His world, to see into that glorious realm of His Kingdom. He wants us to partner with Him for heavenly breakthrough.

God's *yes* together with our *yes* is what brings about breakthrough in prayer. I'm continually amazed that God would choose to partner with us. But at the same time, it makes all the sense in the world that He would want us to join with Him in making history. We are, after all, His children. He is great and all-powerful, but also a loving and caring Father who, I believe, wants to be involved in our lives. Incredibly, He also wants us to be involved in His Kingdom. He wants us to help build His Kingdom here on earth. Some of the prophetic acts that we do come from the Lord, but I think that some of the things that we do are good ideas that the Father says, "Yeah, that's good."

I am convinced that God likes my ideas. So when I pray, I pray from a place of security. It is like I go into prayer believing that God is on my side.

Thank You that, as a child of Yours, prayer is as natural as breathing. I will make space to feel and learn Your heartbeat. I pray that You will fill me with compassion for the lost, love for the world, and increasing wonder at who You are. I say, "Yes!" to all that You are doing in the world. Help me to pray with confidence in who You are and in who You have created me to be.

FOCUSED IN LABOR

When our daughter Leah was expecting her first baby, she asked, with permission from her husband, if I would be the coach for her. I had had three children by natural birth, and she told me, "You're the pro, Mom." It was an honor for me. I told my husband that it was the most amazing experience and the hardest work I've done since I had my own kids.

God is always breaking into our natural world and showing us the spirit realm. That's what happened in this birthing experience with our daughter. In a natural birth, you can invite friends and family into the labor room. Our daughter is a very social being and loved having those friends and family visit up until the time of the birth. As you may know, toward the end of the labor, there is a time that is the most intense. It takes all of your concentration just to make it through the contractions. We were at that place. Whenever a contraction would start, we would release peace over Leah, and then the focus was all on her part to listen to my instructions.

One of our friends came into the room at one of those moments and began talking, not really paying attention to the intensity of what was going on. Leah seemed to be OK with it. After the delivery, I asked her about the distraction in the room. She told me that she really didn't notice because she was so focused on my voice and what I was telling her to do. As she told me that, I had a revelation of intercession. When God gives us strategies to pray—you know, the ones that we burn with—we can become so focused on His voice that we don't become distracted. Nothing can take us away from His voice. There were times during delivery of her own child that my daughter and I would lock eyes as well. It was how she got through the intense times. She drew strength from looking into my eyes. There was an intensity or determination in my eyes that she picked up on, which kept her going.

There are times in our lives when we must stay closer, locking on to His words and His vision. God gives us prayer strategies, and we look to Him for focus and understanding on how to pray with results. Then the birthing will come.

The baby born that day to our son-in-law and daughter was named *Judah* (Hebrew for "praise"). The result of our steadfast focus can only be praise for Him.

I want to lock eyes with You. I want to hear Your voice—Your strategies for intercession—so clearly that nothing else matters. My focus is not on the fear or chaos swirling around me, but on Your steady gaze and Your hope-filled perspective. You have been victorious! Help me to remain anchored in that truth, no matter what.

OFFENSIVE PRAYERS

On a football team there is a defensive team and an offensive team. The defensive team tries to steal the football from the opposing offensive team. The defensive team will try to figure out the offensive team's strategies and plays. The offensive team, however, has the advantage in that they have the ball. With their skill and different plays, they proceed to carry the football down the field to make a touchdown. The offensive team calls the plays, for they have the ball.

For intercessors, it is extremely important to understand that God has already given us the ball. We are the offensive team. If you don't understand that, if you are not praying from a place of victory, then you will be an intercessor whose prayer life is marked with defeat. You will be one who is always trying to protect what God has given you from the devil's plans or, worse yet, running after the devil and trying to figure out what he is doing. How wrong is that? If you do not understand that God has already given you the ball, you will live in fear and pray from a place of lack.

When Joe Montana would throw that ball down the field, he knew right where it was going—right into the hands of his receiver. It was a thing of beauty. What a picture for us of how to live as Kingdom people who know the plays of Heaven.

A good player will be so focused on his target that it feels like there is no one else around. A good player does not just throw the ball around. Similarly, we can't just throw our prayers around here and there.

Like Joe, we are the offensive team. Offensive teams call the plays. They must have confidence that they are going to win. They have to believe that they will win because they know that they control the ball. As intercessors, as the offensive team, our job is to take the land and not to run around after the enemy trying to steal the ball away from him. The devil lost the ball at Calvary.

As intercessors, we need to always remember that we are playing on an offensive team. On an offensive team, the entire team knows where the ball will go and who will catch it. The entire team knows where to run. They have one focus: to get the touchdown. As intercessors, we must listen for the plays that the Lord is calling and pray them in so that the team can catch the ball and make the touchdown. Our job is not to spend all of our time worrying about the enemy's strategies. We are to make the plays that God calls.

Thank You, Jesus, that I am on Your winning team! Thank You that I am not alone in this battle, that I am surrounded in the Spirit by my brothers and sisters in Christ. Thank You that You have gone ahead of us and have secured the victory. Jesus, help me to remember that You are leading me with confidence and strength. You have all authority, and I get to joyfully join into Your victory through intercession.

PRAYING FROM VICTORY

A lot of intercessors spend all of their time worrying about what the enemy will do next, but their job is to focus on God and to partner with His plans. As an intercessor, your job is to find out what God wants to do, which is the opposite of what the enemy is saying. Then you begin to pray what God wants. You don't allow the enemy to bring distraction. You have to make a choice not to partner with fear.

This is how intercessors live an offensive lifestyle. They pray according to God's plans, and they pray from a place of victory.

As a result, we are no longer to be children, tossed here and there by waves and carried about by every wind of doctrine, by the trickery of men, by craftiness in deceitful scheming (Ephesians 4:14 NASB).

When our third grandchild, Haley, was born, her mommy, Jenn, had an infection, and the doctor had to perform an emergency C-section. As they brought the baby out of surgery and rushed her into NICU, they told us that Haley wasn't responding well. They perform a test on babies when they are first born called the Apgar test. It's a number test, ten being the best score. Haley's score was two. We found out later that babies who have a score of two usually don't make it. When they gave us this news, we as a family had to make a decision: Would we agree with this bad news?

I will never forget that feeling. This was our son's first-born. Everything was so new and exciting; then we got this bad report. I remember going and sitting in a chair in the waiting room. I put my face in my hands and asked God what was going on. I heard these words, "It's just warfare. Say 'no'!" So that's what I did. The whole family prayed. This was not to happen. Within ten minutes, the nurse came out and told us that Haley's Apgar was up to seven and that she would be fine. As I write this book, Haley is very alive and well, changing the world around her for Jesus.

You are so worthy of all of my trust, God. You are better than I could ever have imagined. Thank You that following You doesn't mean insecurity. Thank You that I can see clearly the steps before me: I will speak the truth in love, keeping my eyes on You, and following in Your footsteps as I become more and more like You every day. I say, "No!" to every plan of the enemy, placing my trust in Your strong and steady hands.

A NO-FEAR ZONE

Fear has a way of coming up and biting you. Everything might seem to be going great in your life, and you're walking in peace. All of a sudden, fear tries to envelope you, trying to destroy your peace. We as believers have to make a choice to resist fear. When our first grandchild was born and was not doing well, we as a family had to make a choice that we would not partner with fear. The devil has legal rights only if we agree with him. The tool he uses to get us is fear. He does not play fair with us. He will go right for our soft spots.

Do not be afraid of sudden fear nor of the onslaught of the wicked when it comes; for the Lord will be your confidence and will keep your foot from being caught (Proverbs 3:25-26 NASB).

Do you ever just sit back and think about the world, what it looks like now, and what is really going on? Why are things in world events happening? What is really making those events happen? What is the root? Not just on the surface, but deeper—what is making things go the way they are going?

When I look at the world, I can recognize the devil's plan. The root is fear. It really is a simple plan. All the devil has to do is make sure that we walk in fear; then all of our responses will be out of that place of fear. The most repeated command in the Bible is "Do not fear." From Genesis to Revelation, God has repeatedly told us not to fear. God knows our humanness.

When I sit back and look at the world and see what God is doing, it makes me happy. Do these words sound familiar? *"For I know the thoughts that I think toward you, says the Lord, thoughts of peace and not of evil, to give you a future and a hope"* (Jer. 29:11 NKJV).

I will not partner with fear. I see the ways that the devil tries to worm his thoughts into my thinking, but I will trust You, God. I trust that You are thinking about me, that Your thoughts are filled with peace and hope. Thank You, Father, that my safety and security are not in my own hands or in specific circumstances; my peace is found in You alone.

HITTING THE MARK

As intercessors, we need to be focused in our prayers and our strategies. Effective intercessors know how to listen for the plays that God calls, and they know how to catch the ball and make the touchdown. Effective intercessors are offensive intercessors; they know how to hit the mark.

One of the meanings for *intercession* is to "strike the mark." This phrase derives from the Hebrew word *paga*. *Paga* means "to meet"; it is the violent part of intercession. Job 36:32 (NKJV) tells of a violent *paga* meeting: "*He covers His hands with lightning, and commands it to strike* [the mark]."

If we are going to be a people who pray with an offensive purpose, "hitting the mark" in our prayers, we must be on a quest to search the heart of God. How can we do that? Where do we go to find God's heart? We go to His Word to find His heart. I find it interesting that the word *Torah* comes from the root word *yarah*, which means "to shoot straight," or "to hit the mark." God has given us the Bible to show us His heart.

"Eye has not seen, nor ear heard, nor have entered into the heart of man the things which God has prepared for

those who love Him." But God has revealed them to us through His Spirit. For the Spirit searches all things, yes, the deep things of God (1 Corinthians 2:9-10).

In these verses, Paul tells us that we can know the things of God because God has revealed them to us through His Spirit. Paul tells us that the Spirit is searching deeply into the heart of God. No one knows the heart of God except the Spirit. This is where it gets exciting. What we see in these Scriptures is that God is telling us that He has given us the ability to know the things of God. If we dive into the Spirit of God, we can know what is in the heart of God. Wow! God wants us to know Him and to know His ways.

God, more than anything I want to know You. I want to feel Your heart for me, for my family, and for the world around me. Thank You that You want to be known by me! Thank You that it isn't difficult to get to know You. You have given me the gift of Your Word so that I can understand Your heart a little more every day. Help me, Holy Spirit. Illuminate the Scriptures so I might see the goodness of God clearly and accurately.

CANCER-FREE ZONE

One of the targets that we have in our prayers and in all that we do at Bethel relates to our belief that God has promised us a cancer-free zone. That is one of our number-one prayers. We are focused and determined to *hit the mark*. We know that we have the ball on this one. We have seen so many healed of this evil disease. We have also seen people die with this disease. But we know that, as we continue to carry prayer down the field, we will hit the mark and reach the goal.

We know this is a spirit fight. One of the things that we are pushing against is a worldly mindset. I think of a worldly mindset as a humanistic, self-focused, carnal mindset that is not set on the things of God. The more we pray, read the Bible, preach, and "do" by healing the sick, the more we break down that mindset.

Jesus did this very thing. He showed us how to spirit fight. He broke down that worldly mindset by praying, preaching, and doing. One specific way that He broke down that mindset was by healing the sick. If someone you know does not believe that God heals but witnesses a sick person being made whole after you lay your hands on them, this can break through the mindset of the unbelieving heart. We have seen that happen many times—a person who didn't believe in healing became a believer after watching God heal someone.

And do not be conformed to this world, but be transformed by the renewing of your mind, that you may prove what is that good and acceptable and perfect will of God (Romans 12:2 NKJV).

To me, this Scripture is a great example of a heavenly mindset. When our attention is fixed on Him, we are able to see His will more clearly. And when we think with a heavenly mindset, we begin to operate with an offensive lifestyle. You see, God has given us the ball, which is the Word of God; now it is our responsibility to pass it on to others.

There are people I've loved deeply who weren't healed, Father. I have pain and disappointment here, but today I offer up those feelings of loss to You. I open my heart authentically to You. I'm so grateful that I can be honest with You—You're not scared of my anger or my sorrow. But I won't get stuck there. Help me to see beyond my own pain to who You are. Remind me of Your goodness, Your faithfulness, and Your love. I want to continue to carry this prayer down the field until we hit the mark of becoming a cancer-free zone!

WHAT TIME IS IT?

The sons of Issachar knew the signs of the times:

> *Of the sons of Issachar, men who understood the times, with knowledge of what Israel should do, their chiefs were two hundred; and all their kinsmen were at their command* (1 Chronicles 12:32 NASB).

The part about this verse that I like is *"with knowledge of what Israel should do."* The sons had a plan. They not only understood the times, but they also knew what to do about the times in which they lived.

Jacob's blessing to Issachar was strength, rest between burdens, a pleasant land, and life as a burden bearer (see Gen. 49:14-15). In the margin of my New King James Version *Spirit-Filled Life Bible,* it says that Issachar was to be "basically docile, accepting a happy, quiet life in Canaan. They were politically insightful, switching allegiance from Saul to David."

It sounds like the sons of Issachar didn't have a stressful life. They were just a happy people, enjoying their God-given land. I wonder if that's what made them so insightful into the comings and goings of the great nation of Israel.

Their lives were free from worry and stress. They knew how to be happy.

At Bethel Church, my job is to oversee the prayer. As the Prayer Pastor, I get a lot of emails from all over the world. Many of the emails are asking for emergency prayer or have a high prayer alert. Many are good, but many are so full of fear that I must reject the spirit that is attached to them. I refuse to pray out of fear. What I *will* do is just stop and ask God how to pray about the crisis and for His direction. I stay focused on God and not on the crisis. When you move your prayers into fear, you can't possibly get a clear handle on how to pray according to how Heaven is praying. We must be like the sons of Issachar; we must understand and know what to do. Staying focused and keeping to the plan is most important.

Thank You, Jesus, that it is always the right time to experience Your joy and peace. Even in the midst of the most trying circumstances, I can access the joy of heaven. And, in fact, it is wisdom to do so! Thank You that I can see a circumstance most clearly when I am seeing it from Heaven's perspective. My eyes are locked on You, Papa.

DEPENDENT ON GOD

The Old Testament is filled with great stories of kings and leaders of Israel who looked to God for wisdom. Their only hope and salvation was their dependence on what God would do. In Second Kings 18–19 is the story of King Hezekiah and the great Assyrian army. Assyria was located in what is now Iraq. The Assyrian nation, under the leadership of King Sennacherib, began moving south along the coast, attacking and taking city after city. Jerusalem was next on the list to be overthrown. In verse 35 of chapter 18, Sennacherib says:

> *Who among all the gods of the lands have delivered their countries from my hand, that the Lord should deliver Jerusalem from my hand?* (2 Kings 18:35 NKJV)

Hezekiah tears his clothes, covers himself with sackcloth, and goes right into the house of the Lord (see 2 Kings 19:1). Now that's a good plan. Go right to the Presence. From there he sends a scribe, elders, and priests to the prophet Isaiah (see 2 Kings 19:2).

King Sennacherib sends a letter filled with threats to King Hezekiah:

And Hezekiah received the letter from the hand of the messengers, and read it; and Hezekiah went up to the house of the Lord, and spread it before the Lord (2 Kings 19:14 NKJV).

King Hezekiah does a prophetic act. He lays this threatening letter before the presence of God. He reminds God of who He is. It's not that God needs this reminder, but we need to agree with Heaven. This is a good place to start. He asked God to come through for His Jerusalem.

Now therefore, O Lord our God, I pray, save us from his hand, that all the kingdoms of the earth may know that You are the Lord God, You alone (2 Kings 19:19 NKJV).

Isaiah sends back to King Hezekiah and tells him that because he has prayed against Sennacherib of Assyria, God has heard him and will answer (see 2 Kings 19:20). That's a good day in Jerusalem! This story is a good example of living on the offensive. Hezekiah's plan "A" was God. He stayed focused on the ways of God. He understood the importance of being with God, in His presence.

Thank You, Lord, that I can run into Your presence any time something feels overwhelming for my heart. You have made Yourself so available to me. You are my hiding place, my safe shelter. Thank You that, any time a scary situation causes me to forget how mighty and faithful You are, I can run to You and place my worries at Your feet. You are my plan "A."

PRAYER WARRIORS

When we pray from the offensive lifestyle, our prayers are strong and mighty because we have spent so much time with God and He has stamped on our hearts who we are. Out of that relationship of love, we become strong love warriors, taking on the strategies from His heart. We know that, out of our love relationship with our Father, our prayers are mighty. Anything can happen.

God showed me several years ago just how strong our prayers are. In the late '90s, it was really cool to have a sword at church. Many of us felt like having a sword was saying prophetically that we were in a war and that God was fighting for us. We used them for spiritual warfare and making prophetic declarations. All kinds of prophetic acts were done using swords. I was in a conference where we called all the women up and knighted them for the Kingdom. It was a fun time.

I thought it would be really fun to get a dagger. I liked what daggers were used for in wartime. They used them both to fight and to dig out arrow tips that had wounded them in battle.

I went onto a website to order one, and I found one called the state guardian dagger. Prophetically that sounded good to me. I felt like a guardian over my state. I ordered it and waited six long weeks for it to arrive.

During this season in my life, I felt like I was going through a time of deafness in hearing God speak. It was a quiet time. Well, the day came when the dagger came to the house. I couldn't believe how big the box was. It must have been close to six feet high. I thought that they must really pack their goods well. As I unpacked the box, I reached in and began pulling out this very long sword. As I pulled the sword from the box, my spirit ears opened up and I heard, "You think your prayers are like a dagger, but I think your prayers are like this sword."

The sword that I got in the mail that day was a two-handed claymore sword. William Wallace was said to have used this kind of sword as he fought for the freedom of Scotland. They were used in battle. Warriors used both their hands to hold the sword and would control their horses by their legs. There is a place on the sword that has a piece of leather wrapped around it for the second hand. Our prayers are much bigger than we know. The strategies that God gives us to pray are world-changing!

Thank You, God, that the quiet seasons are not seasons of being alone. You are intimately involved in my life in every season. Thank You for this gift of prayer. Thank You that I have direct access to Your heart at all times. Thank You for allowing me to partner with You to see Your Kingdom come. My prayers are powerful!

NOTHING RESTRAINS
THE LORD

To be in an offensive position in this spirit war is very important. You may ask, "Is it important to go somewhere to pray, or can you just pray where you live?" Yes and yes. Most of the time, I have a very strong sense that it is important to go. Many times I've felt that we are going in stealth when we go into an area to pray.

When Jonathan and his armor bearer snuck up on the Philistines, they didn't tell anyone. I'm sure that if Jonathan had let everyone in on what he wanted to do, they would have tried to stop him, or they would have wanted to go with him. The latter would have defeated the whole plan. They would not have been able to go in secret. A lot of the time, our prayers as intercessors are done in secret. Then the prophetic acts that we go out and do are the fruit of our intercession.

King Saul was sitting under a pomegranate tree (see 1 Sam. 14:2). He did not want to take on the Philistines. Comfort was the name of his game. Israel was waiting and wanting their king to fight. Jonathan, seeing all this, had had it. So he with his armor bearer went secretly to take on the whole Philistines' camp (see 1 Sam. 14:6-14). God is looking for intercessors who are passionate for Him and for His Kingdom to come.

Jonathan said to the young man who bore his armor, *"Come, let us go over to the garrison of these uncircumcised; it may be that the Lord will work for us. For nothing restrains the Lord from saving by many or by few"* (1 Sam. 14:6 NKJV).

Don't you love Jonathan's courage and attitude? In saying this, he was making pronouncement over his enemies twofold: 1) you are the enemy of Yahweh, and 2) I carry a great multitude with me today. I am under a covenant with the God of all gods and the King of all kings.

That's the attitude we need in our spirits when we carry out our intercessions. Numbers have nothing to do with what God wants to do in the spirit realm. What matters is just passion and courage. What Jonathan and his armor bearer did that day caused a great commotion, both in the invisible realm and the earthly realm.

When you look at Jonathan in this story, you can see how an offensive life is lived. You can see how nothing is impossible with God. As we carry out those seemingly crazy prophetic acts, choosing to live an offensive life before God, God will fight for us.

I never want to get stuck in my own routine, God.
I want to be humble enough to put my prayers into
action, to go where You are leading. Father, give me
the courage of Jonathan. Help me to know beyond
a shadow of a doubt that You are with me and
that nothing can stand up to Your presence. I carry
a great multitude with me; I am under a covenant
with the King of all kings!

TAKING OWNERSHIP

I consider Redding, California, my home. Not only is it my home, it's my land. I believe that what I pray and speak over my city will make a difference. The same is true for you; where you live is yours. We are spiritual leaders in our land. As intercessors, we need to take that seriously.

Several years ago, there was a brutal murder in our city. Two young men murdered two other men just because they were homosexuals. I woke up that next morning and read the paper to hear that this had taken place in our county. I was saddened by the news. I went up to our prayer house and wept before God. I asked for forgiveness for the murders that we had committed in our city. I cried for mercy, that God would heal our land from the bloodshed.

Because you have plundered many nations, all the remnant of the people shall plunder you, because of men's blood and the violence of the land and the city.... Woe to him who builds a town with bloodshed, who establishes a city by iniquity! (Habakkuk 2:8,12 NKJV)

You see, as an intercessor, it is my job to take ownership over what takes place in this area. You might say, "Wait a minute, you obviously didn't commit the crime, so why are you taking the blame?" Because I have taken "ownership" over my land, I take it personally when something takes place in this area that is sinful and wrong. If something has gone wrong, I see it as my responsibility to make it right through confession and repentance.

I take ownership in the Spirit over my home, my workplace, my city, and my nation in the name of Jesus. I know that You have placed me strategically, God, to bring Your Kingdom to earth in this place. I ask that Your mercy, Father, would flood this land. Send Your supernatural intervention into every area of government, business, and education. Holy Spirit, invade every home and bring Your presence to every family in this region.

THE MINISTRY OF
RECONCILIATION

Many years ago, there was a multitude of First Nations people who were massacred in our area. The massacre occurred long before I was born. I had no part in this horrible atrocity. But because God has placed me in this area, I believe that God has given me the responsibility to contend for this region. Northern California is more than just my home; it is the place I love. As a result, I have become a reconciler, a person who prays for reconciliation, prays for healing to take place in the land. In fact, a reconciler helps to bring people together. *Reconciliation* means "to bring atonement; the act of harmonizing or making consistent; agreement of things seemingly opposite or inconsistent."

Now all things are of God, who has reconciled us to Himself through Jesus Christ, and has given us the ministry of reconciliation, that is, that God was in Christ reconciling the world to Himself, not imputing their trespasses to them, and has committed to us the word of reconciliation (2 Corinthians 5:18-19 NKJV).

The Wintu Indians are the original people group of the Redding area. They are the first landowners of this region. I have come to know several of them, and they are the most wonderful, strong, giving people. Despite all of their wounds, they are a courageous people who continue to labor for tribal recognition by the U.S. government.

God brought a wonderful Wintu Native American woman into my life named Donna. Or should I say I was brought into her life? We sat and talked and prayed together. She taught me about her people. One day Donna came to me and asked if I had heard the saying, "Bury the hatchet." She told me that was what they did when they wanted to make things right, to end a dispute. We had just finished our prayer house but hadn't completed the landscape yet. We decided that we would "bury the hatchet" on the north side of the prayer house. That would be the perfect spot. We took a small group of people, and as a prophetic symbolic act, we buried a hatchet. Donna brought an Indian hatchet, and we buried it right in the ground.

That was one of the first prophetic acts that we did together over our region. Donna, many other intercessors, and I have gone all over our county and prayed and released a cleansing atmosphere. In doing this, we as God's reconcilers are saying, "God, we know that You have given us the responsibility to bring about the ministry of reconciliation, and we are taking ownership of that.

We will do all that You want us to do, when You want us
to do it, and You will show us how to do it."

---

*Father, You have placed me strategically in time,
in location, and in relationship. Thank You that
I have the authority to stand in the gap and bring
reconciliation through the blood of Jesus. Show me,
Holy Spirit, if there are any people in my region
who are in pain due to past hurts. Give me wisdom,
fill my heart with love, and show me how I might
minister Your heart of reconciliation on the earth.*

RECONCILIATION
THROUGH HONOR

I attended a conference in Redding years ago. They had a guest speaker who was a First Nations leader. As he was speaking about helping the First Nations peoples, he mentioned helping out monetarily. I realized that we needed to put our money where our mouth was. We had somewhat of a relationship with the Wintu people through our friend Donna, but that was all. One of our elders in our church was at the conference as well. He emailed us and mentioned that he had heard this same thing at the meeting and thought that it would be a great idea to give to the Wintu tribe.

I called Donna and asked if Bill and I could meet with the Tribal Council. So she made the arrangements. Meanwhile, we arranged a letter to give to the Wintu Tribe along with a check. In the letter, we addressed them as being the first landowners of the Redding area and honored them for who they are. We also explained that Bethel Church, our church, would be giving them a check every month as long as Bethel was around.

That night at the tribal meeting, there wasn't a dry eye in the place. It was a moment I will never forget. The reconciliation that went on in all of our hearts forever changed the atmosphere of our city. Yes, there are still wounds and hurts, but we have friends now, and we continue to pray and help when we are asked. That night at the meeting, many gifts were exchanged. One was a tree that we received from the tribe, a redbud tree. We planted it at our prayer house garden. Since that time, we have received other trees from the tribe as a confirmation of our relationship.

Soon after this gathering, we began seeing the issues of the First Nations peoples being brought up in the news. We saw that there were still struggles but that recognition was beginning to surface. Honor was being given to whom it was due (see Rom. 13:7).

Thank You, Jesus, that You modeled so remarkably the tangible expressions of honor when You washed dirty feet, fed hungry people, and comforted the hurting. Give me Your eyes to see the practical needs around me. Because of You, I have access to the resources of Heaven. So I can freely allow honor to flow to those around me.

A GOOD HARVEST

In Shasta County, there is a two and a half month harvest season for marijuana. Because a lot of Shasta County is remote and in the foothills of the north end of the state of California, there is quite a lot of marijuana grown, not just in our county, but also in the counties all around us. It is a big business. The money that is brought in from the growth of marijuana is, in turn, used to make other drugs.

One of the women in our church told me that one of her sons wanted to talk to me about the drug business in our area. This young man was not saved and was a drug runner himself. I agreed to meet with him and talk. He began to tell me many interesting things about our area and what was going on. It was very informative and gave me some insight that stirred me up for prayer. I asked God to show me how to pray with a strategy.

I like watching the Weather Channel, and I also like to read the weather page in our local newspaper. My husband doesn't understand why I would sit and watch the Weather Channel. I think it must be that the weather is foretelling. It lets you know what is coming. I had been praying about this whole drug ring in our community for about two weeks. One morning I was reading the weather page of our newspaper and noticed a little box with the new moon phases. I had never paid attention to that before, but it caught my eye that morning. That little box showed me the date and times of the full moon and new moon. I mentally put that information into my head and finished reading the paper. When I was done, I picked up my Bible and began reading where I had left off: Psalm 81. I read through verse 4 and stopped. It read:

> *Blow the trumpet at the new moon, at the full moon, on our feast day. For it is a statute for Israel, an ordinance of the God of Jacob* (Psalm 81:34 NASB).

So something stopped me, and I realized that it wasn't a mistake that I had just read about the moon phases in the newspaper and then read about it in the Bible. Sitting there, I knew instantly what I would do. In that moment, I knew what God was telling me to do. It's called the language of the Spirit. It's your spirit man picking up on the movement of Heaven. I felt that I was to go to the north border of our state and blow the shofar at the moon phase at sunrise. We have learned through experience that, when praying at sunrise, there is an open Heaven. It feels like a straight shot right from Heaven to earth.

So having this information, I called a friend, told her what was going on, and asked if she would go with me. We waited until the next moon phase then headed up to the border. We got there right at sunrise and blew that shofar. When we got back into the car, we began to pray. Out of my mouth came these words, "Lord, I ask that You forgive us for allowing a sorcery spirit to come into our region." Deep intercession came on us as we cried for our state, asking God to redeem us and have mercy. As always, we ended in a time of joy and praise. Then we drove home.

That time of year happened to be the harvest time for marijuana crops. A week went by. One day, looking at the paper, I saw our first answer: a drug bust had happened. For the next two and a half months, we watched daily more and more "good" harvesting. Not only that, there were several other kinds of drug busts. There was a U-Haul truck traveling on Interstate 5 just south of us. It got in a wreck, tipped over, and spilled out a methamphetamine lab. Another time a man was pulled over by a highway patrolman for doing an illegal lane change, nothing to be arrested for, but another patrolman pulled up, and he had a dog in his car. The dog was trained in smelling drugs. They opened the man's trunk and found $1.1 million worth of cocaine. This man was on his way to Canada.

By the end of the harvest season, the paper reported that it had been the biggest police harvest of marijuana in the history of Shasta County. I got a call from the young man who gave me all the information. He told me that one of his friends in Canada called him wondering what was going on because there were hardly any drugs coming through.

I have to tell you that, when this young man walked out of the office that day, I told him that he would soon find out who he was. Within two weeks, he came to the Lord and was saved. Eventually, he graduated from our ministry school. Wow! It was a very exciting season of answered prayers rising from one big strategy that worked.

You have real solutions for every problem, Lord. You are not intimidated, overwhelmed, or ignorant of the demonically inspired activity that tries to tear down my community. Show me how You would have me pray, God. Show me how I can partner with You to bring Your light into every dark place. My neighborhood, my city, my state, and my nation were made to bring You glory.

RE-DIGGING THE WELLS

One of my favorite stories on taking ownership in the Bible is in Genesis 26.

There is a famine in the land and Isaac is on his way to Egypt. Along the way, he stops in Gerar. God speaks to him and tells him to stay there and not go down to Egypt. In verse 2, God tells him to live in the land which "I tell you" (see Gen. 26:2). God says in verse 35 that He wants Isaac to dwell in this land, that He will bless Isaac and his descendants.

When God tells Isaac to dwell in the land, God is saying to Isaac, "I want you to stay for a long time. This is your land." For that is what *dwell* means: "to live as a resident." So that is what Isaac did. Isaac also sowed the land. That means he was a farmer. It says that Isaac sowed in that land and reaped in the same year a hundredfold, and the Lord blessed him. The Bible says that Isaac was so blessed and so prosperous that the Philistines who lived there envied him. The king even asked him to move away from them.

In Genesis 21, Abraham had dug a well and King Abimelech's servant had seized the well. Because of this seizure, the king asked Abraham to be kind to him and not hurt him or his people. Upon agreement to this, the two men made a covenant together. The agreement was that the well belonged to Abraham, that this well would be called *Beersheba* (the oath). (See Genesis 21:22-34.)

Now, you might be wondering what is so important about a well. If you have ever been to Israel and traveled to the southern part where Beersheba is, you know how important water is. It is very dry there, but it wasn't only that. Anytime anyone dug a well, he or she was claiming that land surrounding the well. So when Abraham dug the well of Beersheba, he was saying, "This is my land and my descendants' land."

Verse 15 of Genesis 26 tells us that the Philistines had stopped up all the wells that Abraham had dug (see Gen. 26:15). What they were doing—and I believe they knew exactly what they were doing—was hiding any evidence that the land belonged to anyone else. In researching this verse, I found that not only did they fill the wells up with dirt, but they also put dead animals in the wells and made it look like nothing had ever been there. It's interesting that the very thing that was used to make the covenant was the thing used to try to break the covenant.

I think that, while Isaac was sowing the land, he discovered his father's wells. The Bible says that he re-dug all of his father's wells and gave them back their names (see Gen. 26:18). Isaac came into the land, found what was his, and took ownership once again. The story goes on to say that he dug five more wells in that region, that the king came back to him and said, *"We have certainly seen that the Lord is with you. ...Let there now be an oath between us"* (Gen. 26:28 NKJV). Isaac only took back what was rightfully his.

When we pray over our land and re-dig wells—these things that were once places of life—and find new wells of living water, we are doing just what Isaac did. He reclaimed his land; we reclaim our land. Then God will favor us and all will see that favor over us and the land that God has given.

I take authority over my home and my city in the name of Jesus. I speak to the identity of my region, calling out God's purpose for this land. Nothing the enemy has done to undermine the purpose and beauty of my city will succeed. I release restoration, justice, healing, and hope over my homeland. I claim this land for the Kingdom of God!

FOR THE JOY SET BEFORE US

We pastored a church in Weaverville, California, for 17 years. It was a joy for us to raise three lively children in a small mountain community. The church was a family. For several years, whenever Easter would come around, we would have Easter sunrise service and then go to different homes for an Easter breakfast. Especially to our second son, Brian, who at the time was around three years old, food was very important. He loved those special times because there were sweet foods too.

One Easter, we were sitting at the table eating our breakfast, but Brian was having a hard time eating his eggs because he had spotted the cinnamon rolls over on the stove. Reasoning with him just wasn't working. So Bill, being a man full of wisdom, picked Brian up with his plate of eggs, walked over to the stove, and said, "Brian if you eat your eggs, you can have a cinnamon roll."

So Brian sat there in Bill's arms eating his eggs, all the time staring at the cinnamon rolls. When he finished, he got his roll. He had endured the cross (eggs) for the joy (roll) set before him. This may be a silly story, but it does illustrate a good point—i ntercessors should be the happiest people on the planet because they know the plans of God.

God is in a good mood, and He wants to give good gifts to His children. As intercessors, our job is to look ahead to the good gifts that God wants to give to us and to agree with those plans. As intercessors, we have to be OK with the fact that God is OK with motivating us with gifts. We can see this in the Scriptures.

Looking unto Jesus, the author and finisher of our faith, who for the joy that was set before Him endured the cross, despising the shame, and has sat down at the right hand of the throne of God (Hebrews 12:2 NKJV).

Jesus endured so much while He was here on earth, and He endured it for the *promise of joy* that was set before Him. Jesus is into *joy!* We see here that the King of kings and Lord of lords became a man, which was His choosing. And He endured it all for joy. That, in itself, was enough to give Him all of the endurance He needed—enduring the suffering of just being in a man's body after living in the heavenly realm full of light, power, and joy! In my opinion, the joy is what kept Him enduring the earthly living and the dying.

You are the Father of rewards and blessings. I need Your blessing, God. I won't pretend otherwise! You told us that we can expect suffering, but You've designed us to pursue joy and to expect Your reward. I'm so grateful that even Jesus needed to hold on to the joy that had been set before Him to endure the cross. Help me to truly see the joy set before me in this season.

HE'S GOT THE
WHOLE WORLD

We believe, as a people of God's power, that we are to bring Heaven to earth. Joy is a very big part of Heaven. Heaven is filled with joy. It is our responsibility to bring that here on earth.

There is no depression in Heaven, so we have no legal right to depression. If you are depressed, you need to recheck your life. Figure out why, and for Heaven and earth's sake, take care of it. The world needs to see happy, joyful, alive people of God who love and serve out of joy.

If I say, "I will forget my complaint, I will put off my sad face and wear a smile" (Job 9:27 NKJV).

You might be thinking, "But what about all the horrible stuff that is going on in the world? Shouldn't that affect us?" Yes, it should. I met with a woman in our church who wanted to let me know some things that were going on in our city with the occult. After we met, I headed right over to our prayer house. I was feeling a little weighty and needed to get God's perception on all that I had heard.

As I walked in the prayer garden, I had a vision. In the vision, I was in a familiar place with Jesus. We were walking and holding hands, similar to the way that two best girlfriends would hold hands, shoulder to shoulder. It felt like we were sharing intimate secrets. I was talking to Him about the information I had just received. I looked over at His other hand, which was closed. I could tell that He was holding something in secret in that hand. I asked Him what He had in His hand. He opened His hand, and I saw that He was holding the whole world. It looked so small.

When I saw that, all of the heaviness left, and I realized that He has everything under His control and in His hand. Now, that doesn't mean that I don't continue to pray over these matters for my city. But it does mean that I can't carry the heaviness. See, Jesus already did that. He carried it all to the cross.

I am flooded with gratitude, God, that all of the things that seem overwhelming to me never overwhelm You. You are never scared, never hopeless, never shocked by the state of the world or by the state of my heart. Help me, Holy Spirit, to keep seeing this accurately. Papa, would You show me a picture right now of how You see the difficulties that I am currently facing?

RELEASING OUR BURDENS

Because of what Jesus accomplished on the cross, we can now fight *from* victory not *for* victory. Often, as intercessors, we find ourselves praying and begging God for things that are already ours because of what Jesus did on the cross. When Jesus said, "It is finished," can you imagine what happened in all of Heaven and on earth? I can see the demonic realm saying, "Yeah, it's finished and we won," only to be shocked in three days when Jesus overcame death.

Yes, it was finished for the demons of hell. They had to go back to the drawing board and form a whole new plan. But in Heaven, they knew what Jesus was saying. All was complete now—all that Jesus had set out to accomplish on earth, including being that living example to us. He was done.

It's very important that, as intercessors, we have a revelation of what Jesus did while He was here on the earth. Jesus came to set the captive free. He healed the sick, raised the dead, and cast out demons (see Luke 4:18). If we continually carry around an attitude of sorrows, lugging around what Jesus already carried to the cross (all of the sins and feelings that go with that sorrow), then we are denying what Jesus did for all mankind.

Did you notice that I said, "carry"? I'm speaking to those who "carry" the weight and heaviness of another person around even though Jesus already carried it to the cross for us. Jesus said, "It is finished!" My husband has a sermon message with this statement, "What part of finished don't you understand?" If we can catch this thought and put it into our hearts, our prayer lives will change. We will become confident in what Jesus did, and we will become releasers of His Kingdom here on earth.

I'm not saying that there aren't times during deep prayer when we feel and pray with a burden. We can carry this in times of prayer, but I feel that we are not allowed to carry it outside of our intercessions. There is an exchange program for us. We give him *weary, heavy burdens*; He gives us *rest*.

I've noticed that people with a mercy gift seem to struggle with carrying this heaviness more than others. They need to see mercy and justice done, and when it is not, they can carry around the hurt and wounds. You can see it in their eyes. It becomes *unsanctified mercy* because it is carried in human strength. The best solution is to press into God more and to receive His words. When I saw that little world in Jesus' hand, it took all of my fear and worry away.

Jesus, You conquered death! I don't need to be afraid of anything. If I have picked up anything during my intercession that was not mine to carry, I repent and lay it down into Your capable hands right now. Help me to continually release the burden, Lord. I want to take this moment to make an exchange: I take every bit of heaviness, every fear and uncertainty, and I give them to You, God. What do You have for me in exchange?

KEEPING FREEDOM:
THE ANTI-FEAR PLAN

F ear is our enemy. You can pretty much find fear wrapped around any issue in your life that is not centered on the things of the Kingdom. A note about familiar spirits: they are familiar, and at times they are the only things that can falsely comfort us. Therefore, we can feel good in a warped kind of way.

When you have a radical encounter with God, you have new tools to fight back. In the church in Weaverville, my husband led a Friday night prayer meeting. One time, I came late to the meeting. I felt really under it and depressed. We were going through a really big change in our ministry, and I had opened the door to a familiar spirit. I should have known better. I thought that I could feel just a little sorry for myself. That was my mistake. I came into the room and walked right over to where Bill was. He was at the keyboard leading the worship time. I sat right at his feet. He told me later that when I sat down, he looked down at me, and on my leg was a little demon. He reached down to brush it away and it bit him as it left.

Wild, but I believe that demon was a familiar spirit sent to torment me. I understood something that night. As

God gives you freedom, it is your responsibility to keep it. You can't go opening up old feelings and old thought patterns that you walked in under bondage. When you do that, you give permission for the tormenter to come. I did get free that night, thanks to my husband's discernment. This is what Second Corinthians 10:3-5 (NKJV) is talking about when it says:

> For though we walk in the flesh, we do not war according to the flesh. For the weapons of our warfare are not carnal but mighty in God for pulling down strongholds, casting down arguments and every high thing that exalts itself against the knowledge of God, bringing every thought into captivity to the obedience of Christ.

There is much suffering in this world. Jesus suffered. But Jesus knew where His strength was. He had experienced great joy in Heaven. All of Heaven is joy. The Bible says that we will enter into the joy of the Lord one day (see Matt. 25:21). While Jesus lived on this earth, I believe that He knew how to live out of joy, even in the midst of suffering. Remember, Jesus is our perfect example of how to live here on earth. In the movie *The Passion*, there is a scene where Jesus is at His home building a table. His mother comes out, and they are laughing together. That's one of my favorite parts of the movie. I know it's something the writer added to the movie, but I can imagine that that is how Jesus lived. I believe Jesus laughed a lot and enjoyed life. He was able to bring the joy of Heaven to earth.

If we feed ourselves on life and joy and what God is doing here on earth, we will live like Jesus lived on earth. But if we feed ourselves on bad news all of the time, if that is our focus in life, then we will live out of fear and despair.

Thank You, Father, that joy has such an important role in Your Kingdom. I refuse to partner with any spirit—familiar or not—that takes me away from the joy I find in You. Show me, Lord, if there is anything not of You that I have been agreeing with in this season. I want to feed myself on the news of Your great works!

RELEASING HEAVEN'S JOY

I like to imagine. God has given us a wonderful tool—our imaginations. When I read the stories in the Bible, I use my imagination to look at the whole story. What do you see when you read about Jesus healing the sick? Do you see that He healed the sick, or can you see the joy all around Him as He healed?

I know that when we pray for the sick and they get healed, there is a lot of joy around. Everyone is happy. Some get so excited that you will see dancing and celebration. I don't think that it was any different for Jesus and His disciples. When the eyes of the blind were opened and the person who had been deaf all his life could hear for the first time, there was joy and excitement. This is where we need to live. We are releasers of Heaven and all that Heaven holds.

Do you think when Jesus released life over the little girl in the gospel of Mark that there wasn't joy? You can see joy released as you read this story from *The Message*:

But when he had sent them all out, he took the child's father and mother, along with his companions, and entered the child's room. He clasped the girl's hand and said, *"Talitha koum,"* which means, *"Little girl, get up."* *At that, she was up and walking around! This girl was twelve years of age. They, of course, were all beside themselves with joy* (Mark 5:40-42 MSG).

Don't you love that? *"They, of course, were all beside themselves with joy"* (Mark 5:42 MSG). That's the real life of Christ. He brought Heaven to earth, and Heaven is filled to overflowing with great joy. Heaven is just waiting to pour it out on us.

In John 10:10, Jesus says, *"The thief does not come except to steal, and to kill, and to destroy. I have come that they may have life, and that they may have it more abundantly"* (NKJV). Then, in 1 John 3:8, it says, *"The Son of God appeared for this purpose, to destroy the works of the devil"* (NASB).

That should make us all jump up and down with joy. But it gets better. In Matthew, there is a transfer of authority to us! Jesus says:

*All authority has been given to Me in heaven and on earth. **Go** therefore and make disciples of all the nations, baptizing them in the name of the Father and of the Son and of the Holy Spirit* (Matthew 28:18-19 NKJV).

He is handing His authority over to us to *go*. Go do the stuff that He is telling us to do.

Living under Your lordship, Jesus, is not a heavy-burdened life of toil and performance. Your yoke is easy. I follow You with joy-filled obedience, even when things get hard. Thank You for the gift of Your joy! I want to partner with You in every aspect of my life to destroy the works of the devil and bring abundant life. What is one area where You would have me bring Your presence today, Jesus?

EXPORTING JOY

When I began this journey into intercession, I didn't say, "OK, I'm going to be an intercessor now." Instead, I simply fell into the third realm of Heaven, and I fell madly in love with the Holy Spirit. I touched a realm that I had never experienced before. I am now so very addicted to His presence; His realm is where I always want to dwell.

One of the things that we have felt, in all of our travels, is the importance of carrying His joy wherever we go. That is our assignment from Heaven. Remember there is great joy in Heaven, and that is our model for life and ministry here on earth.

> But to the Son He says: "Your throne, O God, is forever and ever; a scepter of righteousness is the scepter of Your kingdom. You have loved righteousness and hated lawlessness; therefore God, Your God, has anointed You with the oil of gladness more than Your companions" (Hebrews 1:8-9 NKJV).

God is speaking about His Son, Jesus, and because He loved righteousness and hated lawlessness, God has given Him the oil of gladness. He had more joy than all of His brethren. He even endured the cross because of the joy set before Him. This tells us that joy is one of Heaven's greatest treasures. God has anointed Jesus with gladness. That word *gladness* is "exuberant joy." That is what our Jesus is anointed with—exuberant joy. We know that Jesus is our example. Therefore, we should carry that same anointing. *Anointing* means, in the Hebrew dictionary, "to smear." In the *New World Dictionary*, the word *anoint* means to rub oil or ointment on. Anointing, that exuberant joy that was poured over Jesus, is what He carried upon Himself.

When we hang around in the presence of Jesus, we will come into contact with that joy. Have you noticed that a couple who has been married a long time begins to look like each other? And they can even act like each other. The more we spend time with Jesus, the more we will become like Him. You want more joy? Do what that psalmist did in Psalm 73. He went before God. He poured out his heart to God; he found God's presence. We need to go before God and stay there until we feel Him and are changed.

Thank You for the gift of emotion, Father. You created me to experience a wide range of feelings. Thank You that I don't need to be ashamed of that or try to hide that from You. You invite me to show up like David—raw, honest, vulnerable—whether I am angry, devastated, or elated. I trust my heart with You. I want to be covered in Your peace, love, and joy.

HEAVENLY-MINDED PRAYERS

Intercessors have the ability to pick up many things that are going on in the spirit realm. Often, it seems like intercessors get so focused on what the devil is doing that they don't look at what God is doing. The question is not, "What is the devil doing?" The question should be, "What is God doing?" This should be the life theme of all of the people of God. But here's the deal. There are times when intercessors can pick things up from the demonic realm. And some intercessors will get stuck here and even live out of this place. They begin living out of the first and second realms.

Let me explain. There are three "realms" that are mentioned in the Bible. The word *realm* means a region, sphere, or area. The Bible specifically talks about the first realm, the second realm, and the third realm. The first realm is the realm that you can see with your eyes. It's the physical realm. "*Now I saw a new heaven and a new earth, for the first heaven and the first earth had passed away. Also there was no more sea*" (Rev. 21:1 NKJV). So here you can see that the first heaven is the earthly realm, or what you can see right now. Our bodies, our homes, and our cities exist in the earthly realm. Deuteronomy 10:14 (NKJV) says,

"Indeed heaven and the highest heavens belong to the Lord your God, also the earth with all that is in it." According to the *New American Standard Exhaustive Concordance of the Bible*, the word *heaven* means, "astrologers, compass, earth, heaven, heavens, and the highest heaven." From the beginning, God created the earth, the heavens, and the highest heavens.

The second heaven, or "midheaven" of Revelation 14:6 (NASB)— *"and I saw another angel flying in midheaven, having an eternal gospel to preach to those who live on the earth, and to every nation and tribe and tongue and people"* —is the demonic and angelic realm where they war with each other. In Daniel, the second realm is also shown to be the demonic and angelic realm (see Dan. 10:13).

Then, there is the third realm. This realm is where the glory of God is. It's the beauty realm. The apostle Paul calls the third heaven "paradise." It's where we can see the great plans of Heaven.

I know a man in Christ who fourteen years ago—whether in the body I do not know, or whether out of the body I do not know, God knows—such a one was caught up to the third heaven (2 Corinthians 12:2 NKJV).

He continues in verse 4, *"how he was caught up into Paradise and heard inexpressible words."*

The third realm is where every believer should live. You see, all believers should live from a place of victory, knowing and partnering with the strategies of God. Ephesians 2:6 (NKJV) says that God has *"raised us up together, and made us sit together in the heavenly places in Christ Jesus."* You have heard the saying, "so heavenly minded, no earthy good"? That's a very impossible saying. I believe that, if you are heavenly minded, you will be of great good to this earth.

Thank You, God, for the gift of sensitivity that You have placed in me. Whenever that gift feels overwhelming, whenever I am picking up all of the frequencies of the first and second heaven, I will turn my face to Yours. I will rise in my spirit above and access Your truth and perspective. Help me to sit with You in the heavenly places.

LIVING UNDISTRACTED

Many intercessors do not live out of a place of joy because they get stuck in the first or second realms. When intercessors get stuck in the first realm, they are preoccupied with logic and reason. Then their prayers become focused on what *seems logical,* which is not where God is coming from most of the time! And then there are those intercessors who get stuck in the second realm. This realm is the dark and demonic realm, which produces hopelessness, doom, and fear.

The problem is that when intercessors choose to pray from those realms, they end up praying from a defensive place. This is what it looks like. You are watching TV or reading the newspaper and some bad news comes across. You have just been made aware of the first realm (the physical realm). You become defensive in your prayers and pray on a human level. Or, you see into the demonic realm. Something bad is afoot. Sometimes it feels like pressure, like you have to pray now. It feels like you are chasing after the devil, and if you don't pray now, the whole world will be destroyed. I know that's a little extreme, but you get the idea.

The devil will be more than happy to let us in on his schemes and strategies if it will distract us from what Heaven is doing.

Let me never be distracted, Father, from what You are doing. I want to face every moment that threatens to overwhelm me with the confidence of Your absolute victory. I will not be distracted. I will remind myself of who You are—of Your authority and Your faithfulness—and I will remind myself of who I am in You.

THE ULTIMATE INTERCESSOR

J esus was the ultimate intercessor, and He saw right though the devil's tricks. When Jesus was led into the desert to be tempted, the devil kept trying to bring Him into a dialogue about His identity. Jesus never went there. The devil was looking for just a little agreement. Don't you get the feeling that Jesus was in complete control of the conversation? He never once gave the devil fuel for his madness.

In the first temptation, when the devil said, "If you are the Son of God command this stone to become bread," he was trying to get Jesus to fight on his terms (see Matt. 4:3). Since Jesus was just finishing up a 40-day fast, it would have been really easy to do just that—turn the stone into bread to prove to the devil who He was. That would have been agreement with the devil. Jesus had no time for this realm of thinking. Jesus didn't even address the identity part of this question. Jesus knew who He was. He brought the situation right into a heavenly perspective: *"It is written, 'Man shall not live by bread alone but by every word…of God'"* (Matt. 4:4 NKJV).

Jesus was completely human while being completely God. He chose this because He wanted to be the perfect example to us. He could have wowed the devil and us by turning that stone into a loaf of bread, but in order to be our perfect example, He showed us a better way to combat the enemy: "Let's bring Heaven in on this. What would Heaven say?" He was always looking in Heaven's direction.

Most assuredly, I say to you, the Son can do nothing of Himself, but what He sees the Father do; for whatever He does, the Son also does in like manner (John 5:19 NKJV).

Jesus, You showed me that I don't ever need to be afraid of the devil's schemes. I will stand on Your Word, I will stand on Your goodness, and I will stand on Your promises over my life. Even when I am feeling weak, I will lean into Your strength. I will get my directions from Heaven.

INFORMED INTERCESSION

When we are focused on the first and second realms, focusing on the devil or those things in life that trouble us, we can get distracted away from the solutions found in the third realm. When we pray or prophesy out of the first two realms, we are not praying according to Heaven. Most of the time, we are praying out of fear. Fear-based prayers are not prayers that will produce a heavenly answer.

Can we know what is going on in those first two realms, or should we completely ignore them? It's OK to know what is going on, especially in the second realm (the demonic angelic realm). It makes us more informed in our prayers. We need to be intentional about getting just enough information to empower our prayer time. We do not live and pray out of those realms. Instead, we need to make sure that we remain focused on God and what He is doing. The key is to always ask God, "Father, what are You doing?"

I remember how excited I was when I began getting into historical research. (I call this prayer mapping.) I loved it! It almost became an obsession because I found myself spending so much time looking into the history of our region. As I began to study and study more, I noticed that I was getting more depressed. Then it hit me, "Oh, I'm getting too much information from the first and second realms and not enough from the third realm." Getting too much information can distract us from what we are supposed to be doing. So I began getting just enough information to be an informed intercessor.

When I am doing research now, I keep myself sensitive, and I can feel when I'm overdoing it. I can tell when I am not focused on the third heaven because the problem starts to look bigger than the answer.

Thanks, God, that I don't have to be afraid of information or bad news. You are ever-present and always available for me to turn to You with what I've learned. Holy Spirit, will You increase my sensitivity toward the capacity of my spirit? I need Your help to guide me to the right sources of information each day. Help me to always keep Your faithfulness and Your power before me.

CONTINUALLY WITH US

Psalm 73 gives great understanding of the heavenly realm. In the first half of the psalm, the writer is looking at those who prosper. He doesn't understand how they can be doing so well.

> *But as for me, my feet came close to stumbling. My steps had almost slipped. For I was envious of the arrogant as I saw the prosperity of the wicked* (Psalm 73:2-3 NASB).

He was seeing through the first level of this world—*the physical realm.* He was looking into the wrong realm. What he was seeing was real, but he needed to understand it from another realm. Then, in verses 16 and 17, it starts to change:

> *When I pondered to understand this, it was troublesome in my sight until I came into the sanctuary of God; then I perceived their end* (Psalm 73:16-17 NASB).

Not until he goes into the sanctuary of God's presence does he understand what will happen to his enemies. Let me explain. In the Old Testament, the sanctuary was where the presence of God dwelt. "*Let them construct a sanctuary for Me, that I may dwell among them*" (Exod. 25:8

NASB). When Jesus died for our sins and was resurrected, the Old Testament ended, and the New Testament began. When that happened, salvation happened. And now the presence of God dwells in us. Wow! How amazing that God would choose to live in our spirit man. We can now access that presence of God within us. We can say with the psalmist, from the deep place of our being, "You are continually with me."

So often I don't correctly interpret what I see in the natural realm. God, keep me humble. Help me to remember that my true understanding always comes through Your perspective. I commit to returning to Your sanctuary—protecting that time in the secret place with You, Father—so that I become more and more aware of Your presence. Thank You for always being with me. I am never facing anything alone.

OUR STRENGTH AND
PORTION FOREVER

When my heart was embittered
And I was pierced within,
Then I was senseless and ignorant;
I was like a beast before You.
Nevertheless I am continually with You;
You have taken hold of my right hand.
With Your counsel You will guide me,
And afterward receive me to glory.
Whom have I in heaven but You?
And besides You, I desire nothing on earth.
My flesh and my heart may fail,
But God is the strength of my heart
and my portion forever.
For, behold, those who are far from You will perish;
You have destroyed all those who are unfaithful to You.
But as for me, the nearness of God is my good;
I have made the Lord God my refuge,
That I may tell of all Your works
(Psalm 73:21-28 NASB).

Y ou can see the psalmist's heart and mind change. You can see the understanding come after he has spent time in the third realm. Your perspective changes; it has to. Everything of weaker value that comes into the realm of God gets discarded. It becomes of no importance. All you want now is Him. You can say like the psalmist did:

Whom have I in heaven but You? And there is none upon earth that I desire besides You. My flesh and my heart fail; but God is the strength of my heart and my portion forever (Psalm 73:25-26 NKJV).

It is not that all of our problems go away as we connect with God's presence, but we have access to a heavenly outlook and we can understand that God has it all under control. This is the place of authority for the believer: "seated in heavenly places in Christ" (see Eph. 2:6). It is not merely a place of divine perspective. It is the place of our enforcement of Christ's accomplishments at Calvary. John 4:35 (NKJV) says, *"Lift up your eyes and look at the fields, for they are already white for harvest."* If we are looking up, we will see it the way God sees it. And God has an answer for everything.

I need You, God. You are my rock, my safe place, my dependable protector. Things may be falling to pieces around me, but You will never fail me. Your loving presence is always with me. You are never intimidated by what I'm facing. Help me see what You see, Father. I need Your perspective on my life!

SPIRITUAL AIRWAYS

Those who own the airways control the atmosphere. The *airways* are the spiritual climate over a city. It is our responsibility to take ownership of the airways and reclaim the atmosphere. When we do that, a shift takes place in the spiritual climate in the region. When that shift takes place, we begin to see signs of revival, and entire cities become transformed by the things of God. When cities become transformed by the things of God, we see more light and less darkness in entire regions.

When I talk about airways, I'm talking about the spiritual climate over a city. There are spiritual powers that rule over cities and regions. These spiritual powers can control the atmosphere. Several years ago, I realized that we were taking control of the airways over our region. We were taking ownership of the atmosphere. Some of the things that we were seeing on our streets, with our ministry teams, included an increase in miracles, transformation in our schools, overall favor, and open doors into our city. There was a unity happening within our city government and the people of God.

In Daniel 10, Daniel received a message, but he needed understanding of the message. He went to fasting for 21 days. At the end of those 21 days, an angel came to him and said:

> *Do not fear, Daniel, for from the first day that you set your heart to understand, and to humble yourself before your God, your words were heard; and I have come because of your words. But the prince of the kingdom of Persia withstood me twenty-one days; and behold, Michael, one of the chief princes, came to help me, for I had been left alone there with the kings of Persia* (Daniel 10:12-13 NKJV).

In Daniel's case, an angel was sent to give Daniel understanding about the message. But the ruling demonic prince held the angel back. He needed Michael, the warring angel, to come and fight this prince of Persia. The messenger angel was sent at the very beginning of Daniel's fast, but it took 21 days for the message to get through (with the help of Michael). There is a very real, invisible world around us, which does affect our visible world.

Thank You, Jesus, that You reclaimed all authority in Heaven and on earth when You rose from the dead. Thank You that You extended that authority to us, the sons and daughters of God. Right now, in the power of Your name, I claim my home, my city, and my region for Christ. I take back any authority that has been, knowingly or unknowingly, handed over to the enemy. And I declare that restoration, transformation, and revival will come to my land!

SHIFTING THE ATMOSPHERE

You will know when you pray with Heaven because when you do you will begin to see changes. We have a ministry school at our church, Bethel School of Supernatural Ministry. I teach one of the advanced ministry training (AMT) classes on prayer and intercession. We meet together, I teach, and then we spend time going out and praying over different parts of our city.

I felt, during one of our prayer journeys, that we were to go to a vacant lot in the city and release a piece of land from a curse. For years this land had been vacant. The property had once housed a bar where a lot of bad things happened. Once, many years ago, a man who was drunk came out of the bar, got in his car, hit a young girl, and killed her. This young girl's father was a friend of one of the men in our church. The man in our church was so grieved over this loss that, driving past the bar on his way home one night, he looked over at the bar and said, "I wish that bar would burn down." That night, the bar burned down.

That happened in the '70s, and from that time on, the lot stood vacant. I don't believe that praying the bar would burn down was the curse. I believe the bar being there and the atmosphere that it brought caused the land to be cursed. One day when I was praying about where to take the students, I remembered this piece of land and the story behind it. I felt like it was time that the curse be lifted off of this property. The land needed freeing.

I gathered the students in a circle and had them declare what God was doing and, through the declaration, release the land from a curse. We believe in doing "prophetic acts" when we are praying. A prophetic act is doing something in the natural realm that brings a supernatural release. Doing an act like this causes an answer to come to the physical realm. So we dedicated the land by pouring oil over it. We gave a shout of praise together that ended our time. I told them, "Now look for the answer."

Within a week, one of the students told me that, a few days after we prayed over our land, a gentleman went to the planning commission of our city and told them that he wanted to develop that land and put homes on the property. That would be evidence of taking the atmosphere. That answer came so fast. By taking our students out that day, two things were accomplished: 1) they were given an accountable and safe environment to explore the ways of prayer, and 2) I believe that Heaven was moved to answer our prayers.

Can you just see what was taking place in the spirit realm? Use your imagination on this one and see what the angels were doing. They were released to do the plans of Heaven. It was like they were saying, "OK, now it's time. The curse has been broken. We now have permission to work." I can see the angels coming to the man who wanted to develop this property and whispering in his ear, "You know that idea you have about developing the corner property? Now is the time to do that."

When you work and co-partner with God, the job gets done. This was one of those times when a clearness in the spiritual communication lines brought quick results. How exciting to see!

Help me to remember to look for Your answers to my prayers, God. Too often, I send up a prayer like a balloon—untethered to the hope of a real, practical response. But I want to live in the expectation, understanding that You are present, engaged, and responsive. It is impossible for me to pray and for nothing to change. You have invited me to partner with You through intercession, not the other way around.

NOT ON MY WATCH

God is waiting for us to take responsibility and to stand up and say, "Not on my watch!"

So I sought for a man among them who would make a wall, and stand in the gap before Me on behalf of the land, that I should not destroy it; but I found no one (Ezekiel 22:30 NKJV).

He saw that there was no man, and wondered that there was no intercessor; therefore His own arm brought salvation for Him; and His own righteousness, it sustained Him (Isaiah 59:16 NKJV).

Don't you love a good challenge? Both of these verses challenge me. To me, they are saying, "What are you waiting for?" Stand up and say to God, "Here; me; I'll do it; I will be the one who stands; I'll be the wall." I don't want God wondering why there is no intercessor. I want Him to be satisfied with what He sees in me. I get excited about that—about standing before God on behalf of injustice and unrighteousness.

There are times in prayer when I feel like I am standing as a wall between God and sin, crying out for God to have mercy. A way to explain this better comes from the days of old when people made fences using vines and hedges. When there was a hole or breach in the hedge, they would have someone stand there to protect the herds from harm until someone would come along to repair the breach.

Therefore He said that He would destroy them, had not Moses His chosen one stood in the breach before Him, to turn away His wrath, lest He destroy them (Psalm 106:23 NKJV).

Here I am, Lord. I will intercede on behalf of my people, repenting for our sins and crying out for mercy. I will be the one to stand in the gap before You on behalf of my land. Thank You that You want to partner with me and that mercy is Your idea.

STANDING IN THE BREACH

As Jesus is the great example of intercession in the New Testament, so is Moses in the Old Testament. There were many times that Moses would stand before God on behalf of a stiff-necked people. Let's look at a couple of those times.

The first story is the story of the golden calf. Exodus 32 tells us that Moses had been up on Mount Sinai and had been there for some time. The people became restless and decided to take things into their own hands. They had Aaron build them a god that would go before them. God could see all that was happening and got angry. He told Moses to get down off the mountain:

> *And the Lord said to Moses, "I have seen this people, and indeed it is a stiff-necked people! Now therefore, let Me alone, that My wrath may burn hot against them and I may consume them. And I will make of you a great nation."*
>
> *Then Moses pleaded with the Lord his God, and said: "Lord, why does Your wrath burn hot against Your people whom You have brought out of the land of Egypt with great power and with a mighty hand? Why should the Egyptians speak, and say, 'He brought them out to*

harm them, to kill them in the mountains, and to consume them from the face of the earth'? Turn from Your fierce wrath, and relent from this harm to Your people. Remember Abraham, Isaac, and Israel, Your servants, to whom You swore by Your own self, and said to them, 'I will multiply your descendants as the stars of heaven; and all this land that I have spoken of I give to your descendants, and they shall inherit it forever.'" So the Lord relented from the harm which He said He would do to His people (Exodus 32:9-14 NKJV).

God had made a covenant with Abraham, Isaac, and Israel, a covenant that God swore by Himself, a covenant to multiply their descendants like the stars. Moses took that covenant and reminded God. Moses stepped into the breach that day. He filled the breach. He repaired the hole in the wall, so to speak. And, because of what Moses said, God changed His mind. Do you hear this? God changed His mind. That's amazing.

God changed His mind because of what Moses said. Moses talked God out of killing the children of Israel. There was a huge breach, and Moses stood there until God changed His mind. I see an attitude in these two stories. We must take a stand and be like Moses. God had given him the promise, and even when God wanted to change His mind, Moses stayed firm. Moses carried faith and mercy with him, and because of that he changed the atmosphere around him.

God, Your humility in this moment astonishes me. You have made Yourself vulnerable and adjustable to Your creation. You so value Your relationship with me that I can remind You of Your promises. Help me to have the confident faith and tender mercy of Moses, Lord. Help me to stand in the breach for my people and change the atmosphere around me.

WITHOUT WORDS

I have found that there are different ways to change the atmosphere. It doesn't always have to be with words.

Behold, as the eyes of servants look to the hand of their masters, as the eyes of a maid to the hand of her mistress, so our eyes look to the Lord our God, until He has mercy on us (Psalm 123:2 NKJV).

Look at the last part of this verse. They were just keeping their eyes on the Lord. No words were necessary. Just keeping focused on the Lord *until*.

We have many beautiful mountains around our city. One time we were heading to the top of one of them just to pray over our city. I had been wondering how we would pray when we got up there, asking God if there was anything I should bring to use as a prophetic act. I had made a shawl from purple material and a gold cord around the edges. I decided to take that shawl up to the top of the mountain.

The view from the top of this mountain was breathtaking. There was a lookout right at the top, and you could almost see all the way around the mountain from this spot. It was a gorgeous day. There was a breeze blowing. That day, all I knew to do was to stand at the edge of the mountain and lift up my purple shawl and let it blow in the wind.

So, there I stood with both hands up over my head, holding my purple shawl and letting it catch the wind. Doing this was a physical prophetic act. For me, the color of purple is royalty and intercession. The gold cord was the glory around the royalty and intercession. As it blew in the wind of God, it was releasing over a region the royalty, intercession, and glory of the Kingdom. I know— it sounds a little crazy, but it sure felt good, and it was really fun.

You might ask, "Did you really have to do that?" Well, maybe not, but I think that God likes what we do for Him, even if it looks a little crazy sometimes. Doing these acts may seem crazy or super spiritual to peers, but in doing these acts I believe that we are standing as intercessors and that we are changing the airways around us.

Holy Spirit, please come and fill my imagination, inspire my thoughts as I press into intercession. Any thought that is not of You I release, and I trust that You will guide my prayer time. Thank You for an increased boldness as I move in prophetic acts, and thank You that this gets to be fun, creative, and filled with Your freedom.

WARFARE WORSHIP

One day I was teaching in our supernatural school about intercession. At the end of my teaching, I asked if there were any questions. One of our young men, who we would have come up on the platform from time to time to dance during our worship, made the comment that he didn't think that he was an intercessor. I looked at him and said, "Are you kidding me?" I told him that he was an intercessor and that his intercession was the dance. You see, his idea of an intercessor was one who just used words to intercede. I explained to him that there are different types of intercession and that when he danced he was interceding. I told him that his intercession was the worship that became the warfare.

Two elements in warfare that I feel are our greatest tools of intercession are worship and joy. I believe that these two weapons bring more confusion to the devil's camp than anything else. Both of these weapons of war come out of our intimate relationship with our Father God.

The Greek word for *worship* is *proskuneo;* it means "to kiss." It is a feeling or attitude within us that keeps us close to God. It is not just about coming to church on Sunday and singing songs during the worship service. Even though that is an important thing that we do together, it is not the most important thing. Worship comes from within us and goes with us throughout our day. When we adore God, we are kissing Him.

Warfare worship is coming in on God's terms, not the devil's. We are focused on God, which ushers His power and presence into our intercessions.

I was in one of our worship services one Sunday morning, and I kept getting distracted in my spirit. I felt like there were some witches in the room. I found myself completely out of worship. I remember, I kept turning around to look to see if I could figure out what was going on. I did this a few times. Then I heard Holy Spirit whisper, "You are being distracted from Me; just worship Me." It was a little nudge from the Spirit, but I got it. I realized that what I needed to do was just be with God and worship. He would take care of the spiritual matters in the room.

My weapon of warfare that morning was to worship Him. God once spoke audibly to my husband saying, "He watches over the watch of those who watch the Lord." It is clear that having our eyes fixed on Him is our most responsible position, as God watches over the things that matter to us.

Holy Spirit, would You show me the ways I might already be interceding on a daily basis without even being aware of it? Thank You, Father, that Your first language isn't English. Thank You that You see my heart and that my prayer can take many different forms as I pull close to You throughout my day. Help me to become more aware of Your constant presence.

TERRIFYING THE DEMONIC

When we worship, we have access to the heavenly realm. When we worship, we push ourselves out of the inferior realms where we can pick up all of the negative stuff, and we end up in the glory realm, surrounded by His presence. I heard a story many years ago about a Christian man who was very depressed. He was so desperate for God to help him. He was crying out to God one day and heard the Lord tell him, "For a whole year, I want you to worship me." God went on to tell him that He didn't want him to ask for anything when he prayed. Just worship. After that year, he was released from the depression that he had lived in for so long. I'm sure he learned a very valuable lesson in that year.

Someone asked my husband what his prayer life looked like. He said, "If I have an hour to spend praying, I will usually worship for around 45 minutes and pray the rest." It's amazing how many things you can pray for in ten to fifteen minutes.

Worship, whatever form—dance, adoration that comes from our mouth, or any other kind of worship—terrifies the demonic realm. I believe they cannot stand to hear or even be close to those who are true worshipers. I've watched our son Brian take his guitar and play over a person in torment to see peace come. I know of a woman who goes to the convalescent hospital in our city and plays her flute over Alzheimer's patients to watch them become peaceful.

God, I come into Your presence today and I consciously drop every heavy thing I've been carrying at Your feet. I release any pain, worry, and confusion that I've picked up from the inferior realms. I will drop those burdens and, instead, choose to worship You. Worship is my weapon, spending time with You is my life source.

FREELY AND LIGHTLY

I believe we are to be people who have Jesus' joy full in us. We are to be like that in every area of our life and ministry. One of the missing elements I see in many of those who are interceding is that they need their lives filled up with heavenly joy. I would love to go to Heaven for a visit and see just how joyful Heaven is. Their intercession in Heaven is not one of labor and work. There is none of that in Heaven. I think the intercession of Heaven is from a place of joy, a place of knowing.

For My yoke is easy and My burden is light (Matthew 11:30 NKJV).

The Message says it this way: "*Keep company with me and you'll learn to live freely and lightly.*"

One of the men in our church came to me with a dream he had. He told me that he saw a river, and over the river a group of women and I were walking suspended. We came floating over the river, laughing and filled with joy. We were taking care of problems with laughter and joy. It wasn't hard. There was a lightness to what we were doing. Along the riverbank there were broken crystal vases. We had a supernatural vacuum cleaner and just came along and vacuumed the brokenness away. He said that as he watched us, it seemed light, and we made it look so easy. I just laughed and said, "Yes, that's how we pray."

To some, that may seem like an impossibility. I would tell you that it is the most refreshing and effective way to war. One of the tricks of the enemy is to get us on his level, to get us to live on his playing field. Satan's world is full of labor and striving. If we step into that realm, we will only experience burnout. That's the plan of the enemy, to wear us completely out. It's not that we don't continually keep praying; it's our attitude in the continual prayer. Is there a striving in our prayers where we are doing all the work? Is there a weight that we carry around?

God wants to remove the stress and the striving from our intercessions. We need to keep filled up so that we won't burn out.

God, my confidence rests in Your trustworthy hands. I want to be so connected to Your heart that I look at every problem with joy, hope, and expectancy. Thank You, God, that I don't have to make these feelings up, but that they are the natural byproduct of growing to know Your goodness more and more. I say "yes" to living freely and lightly with You!

CONFUSING THE DARKNESS

When you use joy in your warfare, it is because you are expecting good to happen. I took my interns to a Buddhist monastery in our area. I thought it would be a good experience for them to pray in a place where another god is served. We went there to pray. I had been to this place several times before and had found that it was an easy place to pray. When we got there, I told them to just walk around and begin praying and feeling what God wanted to do. While we were having this time of walking, one of my interns came leaping by me, smiling and giggling. I like to call her Tigger. I love to pray with her because she is always finding God's heart. She told me in a singsong voice that there were a lot of demons here and that it was really easy to pray.

When you experience God's presence around you, even in a demonic setting, you can find it easy to pray. Needless to say, we had a great time praying together that day. When you carry the joy of the Lord with you, all kinds of things happen. Joy brings excitement to the air, and it releases life. Really, it releases all of Heaven. I find myself, in the darkest places, getting so excited over what I sense God wants to release over a place or over a situation. We are releasers. We're meant to overcome the darkness with light. Do you want to bring confusion to the darkness that is trying to rule over you and others?

In Him was life, and the life was the Light of men. The Light shines in the darkness, and the darkness did not comprehend it (John 1:4–5 NASB).

That means that the darkness cannot overtake the light. It doesn't understand it. Darkness looks at light and gets all confused. Just knowing that when you pray will give you a joy that will burst from you. The New King James Version *Spirit-Filled Life Bible* says, regarding the word *comprehend*, "The Christian's joy is in knowing that light is not only greater than darkness but will also outlast the darkness."

Thank You, Father, that there is no battle between light and the dark. As soon as the light enters a situation, darkness dissipates. Thank You that it would be impossible for darkness to overwhelm Your light. Father, will You show me right now what Your light looks like entering the darkness of whatever situation I am facing? I want to be filled with Your joy.

LAUGHTER IS GOOD MEDICINE

Warfare through joy is like the element of surprise on the battlefield. I believe that this joy brings confusion to the enemy's camp. The enemy doesn't know how to combat joy in a person. This joy catches the demonic realm completely off guard.

We have a prayer meeting at our church on Sunday night before the service. It's called our preservice prayer. I love to watch the visitors come to this meeting. It really should be called the happy prayer meeting. When you come into the room, you will be met by people who are sitting, lying on the floor, or walking in a circle around the room. Some people will be walking with their arms around their friends, some will be lying on the floor soaking in His presence, others will be sitting and reading their Bibles.

The reason I like to watch the visitors is because I don't think that many of them have ever been in a prayer meeting quite like this one before. Sometimes it appears that they don't know what to do or how to act. It's definitely not a time for being serious. It's a time for joy in the house. Usually, by the time we finish, there are people all over the floor, and better yet, laughing people all over the room. We feel that the angels really like that atmosphere and seem to show up and have fun too. The way we fight is a lot of joy! Laughter is good medicine.

A merry heart does good, like medicine, but a broken spirit dries the bones (Proverbs 17:22 NKJV).

Thank You, God, that being in Your presence means being in the presence of peace, joy, freedom, love, hope, and heavenly solutions. How could I not feel delighted when that is my reality? Thank You that being joyful in the face of trial does not mean that I don't care; it means that I care so much I've brought my care to the safest, most capable place in the universe—Your hands.

INTERNAL REST

I remember one time when I felt as though I was carrying so much responsibility in prayer. At that time, I had one of our students come up to me one day and tell me basically that it was all right, that I didn't have to feel or carry all the responsibility of prayer. That word was so encouraging to me that day because that was what I was walking in at that moment. It hit me like a breath of fresh air. I received the word and came back into a place of rest. It doesn't mean that I stopped praying for what was on my heart. But it took me out of the striving and performance that can wrap itself around our prayer agendas. Faith is more the product of surrender than it is of striving.

There is a mindset of performance that can grab hold of us and push us to do things for God that He is not asking us to do. When that happens, it takes us right out of rest. We can feel like we need to do for God so that He will approve of us. We think by doing this God will accept us more and maybe love us more. I'm telling you, you don't have to do a thing for God, and He will love you no less.

So many of us have believed that we need to labor and perform for God so that we can gain an identity, so that we might be accepted. But in the Kingdom we start off accepted. From there our identity is formed. As intercessors, we need to pray out of that new identity, that core belief that says, "I am already accepted! I am already loved! I already have favor with God!" You see, we are already accepted. Unfortunately, many of our life experiences do not teach us this. In life, you get rewarded or receive approval if you do this or that. The Kingdom of God doesn't work that way. God is not sitting up in Heaven waiting to love you if you will do something for Him. He is a lot more interested in our entering into His love and rest.

I get to partner with You, Father, to see Your Kingdom come into every area of my life and every sector of our hurting world. But today, I remind myself that breakthrough does not rest on my shoulders, that You are not dependent upon me to supernaturally invade, and that I do not need to labor or perform for You. I am already loved and accepted by You, and I'm so grateful for that, Lord.

TRUE SABBATH

True Sabbath becomes the rest of God. As God rested, and then as Jesus finished His work and rested, we too can enter into a true rest.

There remains therefore a rest for the people of God. For he who has entered His rest has himself also ceased from his works as God did from His (Hebrews 4:9-10 NKJV).

The meaning of the word *rest* in both the Hebrew (*shabath*) and Greek (*katapausis*) is to "cease, celebrate, desist from exertion, leave, put away, reposing down, and abode." I believe that the true Shabbat rest means to cease from your labors, your own efforts, your own activities. I am not implying that you stop your ministry or working for the Kingdom. What I am telling you is that you must have the heart of rest.

True rest means ceasing from your own efforts, your own striving, and depending on the works of another—God. Whenever I begin to get that overwhelming feeling and I feel the striving coming on, I stop myself and enter right back into the rest of the Lord. When we walk in this rest, we live our lives more fully, and we are more effective in our ministries and giftings. As intercessors, if we want to stay in a place of rest, we have to learn how to pray and do our part and to then give our burdens back to the Lord.

Our daughter, Leah, was a nanny for five years. She started overseeing two girls who were amazing. One of the little girls could see into the spirit realm. She was able to use her sense of feeling and her sense of seeing to understand what was going on. I called Leah one day and asked if they could go out to eat. We met at one of the local restaurants for lunch. As we walked into the restaurant we noticed that (we will call her) Rachel started hiding behind Leah. When we got to the table, she was pretty disturbed and kept turning around. I asked her what was the matter. She told me that the lady sitting behind us was sad, that her heart hurt. Rachel was only three at the time. I realized that Rachel was seeing into this person's life.

So we prayed right there and asked Jesus to help this lady and heal her heart. Rachel was still upset. So I told her that we would pray one more time. We did, and then I told her that we had to give this feeling to Jesus and let it go. We did, and Rachel was fine and returned to her happy self. I sat there amazed and thought to myself, "I wish that I could have learned that lesson when I was young. That lesson would have saved me a lot of internal heartache."

Because I know Your goodness, because I have surrendered every aspect of my life to You, I can return to this place of trust-filled rest. Rest is my home base in You, Lord. Help me to feel acutely any time I have left Your rest and am riding on my own strength. Increase my childlike dependence on You, Papa.

THE REST OF THE LORD

God is not asking us to carry the world on our shoulders. He is asking us to enter into a rest that is internal. My husband is, I think, one of the busiest people on the planet. It is a challenge for him to get the rest he needs. But the one thing that I have noticed through our years together is that he carries an internal rest of the Lord. It is very strong in him. He knows where his source is, and he draws from it often. If he didn't have that inner strength, there is no way that he could carry on with his life. We have no plan "B." God is our plan "A," and He is our source.

Come to Me, all who are weary and heavy-laden, and I will give you rest. Take My yoke upon you and learn from Me, for I am gentle and humble in heart, and you will find rest for your souls. For My yoke is easy and My burden is light (Matthew 11:28-30 NASB).

Rest is mentioned twice in these verses. The first time Jesus is saying, "Come all who are weary and heavy and I will give you rest" (see Matt. 11:28). The second time He tells us, "You will find rest" (see Matt. 11:29). We come to Him first, and He gives us that rest. Then, as we continue to take on His yoke, we will learn from Him. It's the school of the Holy Spirit that we have entered into. As we grow in Him and His ways, or even His presence, we will then find rest for our souls.

But even though we can carry the rest of God with us, we still have to learn how to enter His rest. I remember one of the first times that I began to practice moving into the rest of God. It was a few years ago, and I had driven into town to do some shopping. On that hour-long drive, the vehicle that I was driving decided to give up and quit. My first response was to panic and get really mad. "How could this happen? Everything is now messed up for the day." You know how we carry on sometimes.

I found a pay phone (no cell phones then) to call my husband. As I began to dial the number, I thought to myself, "Why am I acting this way? Why am I so upset?" Then I realized something that was so simple but that changed my life. I thought, "You know, I think that if I settle down and come to rest inside, I will be able to see what God can do in this situation." So I made a simple choice and decided to let God have this little mess of a day. Of course, once I made that decision, everything lined up and worked together. I chose the "rest of the Lord" that day for my life. I think about that day often. In what seemed like a trivial thing, God let me see that I could draw from His rest anytime I needed. It was my choice.

You do not demand striving or performance from me, God. The closer I get to You, the more I realize the truth of those verses in Matthew—Your burden is light; in Your presence, I find true rest. Help me, Holy Spirit, to feel when I am moving out of rest and into striving. I want to live from the rest of the Lord in every circumstance.

WHAT ARE YOU DOING, GOD?

As a leader in intercession in our environment, there have been times when people have started to pick up on negative things more than others. I think of "negative things" as dreams, visions, and thoughts that do not reveal the plans that God has to bless the earth. During these times, people pick up dreams, visions, and thoughts from the second realm.

During one such time, I felt like we were not seeing correctly as intercessors. When I went to the Holy Spirit for counsel and understanding, I felt like He told me that He was allowing this information to come out because He wanted us to learn how to pray from Heaven's perspective. So when people would come to me with the negative, second realm feelings and insights, I would tell them that God was allowing them to see this for a reason. It was now their responsibility to see this from Heaven's perspective.

I told them that they needed to ask God what He was up to. You see, when you see something negative, you always need to go to God and say, "OK, God, what are You doing? What are You saying through this? How do You want me to pray?" It is always easy to find dirt. But

God wants us to look past the dirt and to look for the treasure. The Scriptures say, "*It is the glory of God to conceal a matter, but the glory of kings is to search out a matter*" (Proverbs 25:2 NKJV).

It's so easy to see what's wrong in the world. I turn on the news, and all I see is the brokenness and heartache that surrounds me. But God! Lord, I turn to You with all of it. With every piece of negative information, I will shift my gaze back onto You. I will exchange the pain for Your perspective. I will leave my worry and fear at Your feet and, instead, pick up Your joyful plan for redemption.

FINDING THE GOLD

One Sunday morning, I found myself on the floor with God. He brought a picture of a man who owned one of the tattoo parlors in town. I had seen this young man at his shop one day. I could read him by just looking at him. The eyes tell you all you need to know. That Sunday morning, I saw hate and anger. Instead of cursing the man and cursing his business, I began to see God's heart for him.

Oh my, I was so undone. I prayed his destiny over him and prayed for God to pour His love out on him and to take the hate and anger. I have never heard if that young man changed his ways or if the hate and anger left. But because of the intense time of prayer, I know that God was up to something that morning. I was the one standing in the gap for that man, pleading his case before God. Allow God to grab your heart. Let Him take you to a place of intercession. Be still and know that He is God. When I was praying for that young man, I was seeing him the way God saw him. It's what we call "finding the gold in someone."

In finding the gold in someone, you have to dig deeper. It's never hard to find dirt, but we must go deeper to find the gold; that's seeing a person the way God sees him or her. When we see bad stuff around us, all we need to do is go deeper in God and find the gold. Find the things that God is saying. Then we can come into agreement with the gold. Wow! What a concept, praying Heaven!

Father, it's so easy for me to feel compassion for some people and so challenging with others! But I know that Your heart is filled with tenderness, mercy, and love toward each one of us. Show me Your heart for one difficult person in my life, God. How do You see him/her? What do You love about that person?

INTERCESSORY TOOLBOX

Our church, like most churches, had a monthly tradition of taking Communion as a congregation. All those who knew Christ as their Savior celebrated the death and resurrection by sharing in Communion. As a young girl, I thought the best part of this was that I got to eat a little wafer and drink a doll-sized cup of juice. That was pretty fun! At that time, I was getting to participate in the joy and celebration of Communion, but it would be many years before I began to fully experience and understand the power of this tool that Jesus gave us. In fact, it was really only a few years ago, when my husband became so ill that his life appeared to be in jeopardy, that I began to understand Communion in a whole new way.

In First Corinthians 11:23-26 (NKJV), Paul writes:

For I received from the Lord that which I also delivered to you: that the Lord Jesus on the same night in which He was betrayed took bread; and when He had given thanks, He broke it and said, "Take, eat; this is My body which is broken for you; do this in remembrance of Me." In the same manner He also took the cup after supper, saying, "This cup is the new covenant in My blood. This do, as often as you drink it, in remembrance of Me." For as often as you eat this bread and drink this cup, you proclaim the Lord's death till He comes.

In the midst of His betrayal and impending death, Jesus gave us a tool. He gathered His disciples around for the Passover meal, He gave thanks, and then He gave all believers a way to remember the New Covenant that was about to be made on the cross.

I have always taken Communion whenever I have felt prompted by the Holy Spirit. As an intercessor, I have included Communion as a part of my prayer time. It has always been wonderful and powerful. However, it wasn't until Bill got sick several years ago that I grabbed on to Communion in a more intentional way. Something shifted for me. Since that time of taking Communion daily in the hospital with Bill, I don't wait for Communion Sunday at church or even for the Lord's nudging. I've started to take Communion as a tool in my intercessory toolbox, as a purposeful and proactive part of my relationship with the Lord. I usually take it every day, sometimes multiple times a day, and this new intentionality has shifted my expectation and understanding of the power behind that little wafer and small cup of juice.

Thank You, Jesus, for giving us the gift of Communion. Thank You for showing us this powerful tool of remembrance that we can use in our intercession any time. I never want to forget Your broken body or the blood that You shed for us. Help me to remember.

SEASONS OF PRAYER

On Sunday, April 9, 2017, our church body ended a corporate fast. My husband preached a wonderful sermon on the impact of Communion, and at the end of the service we took Communion as a congregation. We prayed together, applied the blood of Jesus to our families and communities, and celebrated what Jesus did for all mankind. That morning, I prayed—like I always did—for each of my family members. But I also felt moved to pray for two of my best friends' children who were lost in their spiritual lives. I pleaded the blood of Jesus over their lives and remembered all that Jesus had done for them when He went to the cross. Even after we were finished taking Communion, though, I couldn't shake the feeling that I was supposed to keep praying for them.

Sometimes the Lord invites us into what I like to call seasons of prayer. These are moments in time when something or someone is put on our heart to pray for, and we just can't let it go. In those seasons, the Holy Spirit will press upon us to keep praying for that specific person or issue. This intense focus may last just a day or much longer. And in that time of prayer, we may get to see the answer to our prayers, or we may just be invited into the process without seeing any specific results. But either way, we continue to pray because we are being pulled to do so. And usually, just as quickly as the season of prayer comes, it will lift.

Praying for the children of my friends lasted for several days. At the end of that time, I knew that I was released from that season of prayer when these two individuals were lifted from my heart. Not that I didn't still love and pray for them, but they weren't constantly in front of my face. Even though there hasn't been a conclusion to their story yet—these two are both still on their journey back to the Lord—I know that that time of praying for them intentionally and taking Communion, pleading the blood of Jesus over their lives, was fruitful. In these moments, we may not always be able to see the direct results of our prayers, but we can rest assured that another seed was planted.

Any time we are entering a season of prayer for an individual or an issue, we are co-laboring with God. When I use Communion during these seasons of prayer, I joyfully get to do my part in declaring Heaven over their lives. God's got them. I just get to be on the winning team.

Who would You have me pray for today, Lord?
Will You bring someone specific to mind? Help me
to know how to pray, God, and give me the grace
to intercede for that individual until that season of
prayer comes to an end. I want to pray with Your
heart, God. Show me what You are doing in this
person's life.

COMMUNION PROPHESIES

When we use Communion as a tool for intercession, we are not only realigning ourselves with Christ, but we are also proclaiming the reality of Heaven over every area of our lives. When I take Communion, I take it as a prophetic act, applying it to any situation that is weighing on my heart. A prophetic act is a Holy Spirit-inspired physical action that disrupts the atmosphere. Sometimes, I'll feel as though God wants me to do something tangible to activate something that I'm praying into. During those moments, I simply ask the Holy Spirit, "What should I do about this?" Then, I'll feel prompted to—for example—take my shofar into the prayer house that we have at Bethel or go to a specific place to take Communion. In completing the prophetic act, we are releasing something into the atmosphere that helps the answer to our prayer to break through.

In Exodus, God had the Israelites kill a lamb and put the blood over their doors, signaling to the Spirit of God to pass by without harming the family inside. Moses instructed the Israelites:

You shall take a bunch of hyssop and dip it in the blood which is in the basin, and apply some of the blood that is in the basin to the lintel and the two doorposts; and no ne of you shall go outside the door of his house until morning (Exodus 12:22 NASB).

The physical lamb's blood didn't save them; the will of God saved them. But the families that participated in this prophetic act were revealing a heart submitted to God. The lamb's blood was a prophetic act that each family did in order to align themselves with God's will and alert the spirit realm as to whom they belonged.

When Jesus led the disciples through Communion, during their Passover meal together He was creating and modeling a prophetic act that believers could continue implementing. He was giving us a way to align ourselves with Heaven and bring Heaven's reality to earth. Often when I take Communion, I prophesy to myself. There is something powerful in the spirit realm about the declaration of truth, so I talk to myself out loud. I remind myself who I am, that I'm a daughter of the King and that I'm strong in Him. I pull on the promises of the Bible as they come to mind. I'll say, "I am crucified with Christ" (see Gal. 2:20). I let the reality of the New Covenant wash over me, changing any mindset within me that needs to be changed. I declare over myself, "I have the peace that passes understanding" (see Phil. 4:7). I remind myself that I can walk in His peace no matter what circumstances surround me.

Thank You, Jesus, that because of Your blood I am free and forgiven. I belong to the Almighty God, Creator of Heaven and earth. I am loved beyond my wildest imagination. I have been chosen and fought for every day of my life. I am God's treasure.

THE FINAL WORD

We are at war. We never want to concentrate on anything the devil is doing. We know he's already been defeated! But there is a war constantly going on all around us. We never need to be distracted by the activity of the enemy. But we can be aware of the battle that is going on all around us for our minds, for our authority, for our health, and for our peace. We have the winning hand every time!

Every time we take Communion, we remind ourselves that the devil has been defeated. The cross had the final word. But I think everyone has experienced being attacked. I have dealt with health issues, and there are moments when I've been slammed spiritually. I have had to really lay hold of God's promises of peace. I've always considered myself a peaceful person, but I have had to honestly ask myself, *Do I really believe that I can walk in peace when there are so many things attacking that very thing?*

When I'm taking the bread and the wine in a moment like that, I am in a spiritual battle for my health—spirit, soul, and body. Especially when there's something going on in my world that is threatening my wholeness, it's important for me to take Communion more than once a month. It allows me to continually remind myself who I am, who Jesus is, and what He did. Through Communion, I am brought back to the realization of reality: His world is my true reality, not this one.

There's an old hymn I remember singing as a girl, and the words still ring true. "There is power, power, wonder-working power in the blood of the Lamb. There is power, power, wonder-working power in the precious blood of the Lamb." There is enough power in His blood to cancel any curse, to save us from our sins, and to heal our bodies. And that power has not waned in 2,000 years; it is very much alive and well.

Holy Spirit, it's so easy for me to forget that there is a war raging in the spirit realm. Will You help me to remember that my fight is not against other people, but against the powers and principalities of darkness? Today, I take Communion, reminding myself that the same power that raised Jesus from the dead has not changed. There is wonder-working power in the blood of the Lamb!

CUTTING A COVENANT

Why is Communion so powerful? We've heard of wonderful testimonies surrounding Communion—people being healed, couples who were dealing with infertility taking Communion every day and getting pregnant, and of people falling out in the middle of taking Communion. They had an encounter with the Lord that was so powerful while they participated in the sacrament that their bodies could no longer stand up. That's more than just a wafer and some grape juice. That's the power of the Living God.

To understand more about the power behind this, we need to go back and look at covenant. Communion is the reminder that Jesus Himself gave to us the ultimate covenant. It is the body and the blood of Jesus, shed for us.

Blue Letter Bible tells us that the Hebrew word for covenant, *beriyth*, is rooted in a word that means "to cut" or "to eat." Within the expression "cutting a covenant" itself is the graphic depiction of how a covenant was made. When two individuals were cutting a covenant, the ritual included taking a sacrificial animal and dividing the animal into pieces. The two parties would then walk through the scattered carcass, swearing an oath of allegiance in the midst of a path of blood. Essentially, the two parties were making a public declaration that it would be preferable to be like the dismembered animal beneath their feet than to break this promise.

Each blood covenant was a promise of connection, protection, and provision. Like a marriage covenant, where two people are joined into one, the blood covenant created a bond that superseded all other realities. And this was done through the shedding of blood, a public expression that involved the most intimate aspect of life—the blood flowing through our veins. Blood carries and sustains life. Each blood covenant offered a promise that would enhance life, but it came with the potential cost of life.

There is an old sheep-farming tradition called lamb grafting. If a ewe (mother sheep) loses her baby to sickness or another tragedy, she will refuse another orphaned lamb, despite her plaintive cries after her lamb's death. Her baby has a specific scent, and she will reject any baby that's not her own. The farmer, however, can take the skin of her dead baby lamb and drape it over the back of the hungry orphan, covering his old smell with the familiar scent. The ewe, thinking that she is smelling her own baby, will accept the orphaned lamb and the baby will survive. Covenants are a covering for those involved. And no one has made greater covenants with His people throughout history than our God.

I know that I can fully trust Your promises to me, God. You are so faithful, so mighty, and so good. Even after Adam and Eve had sinned and were no longer able to stay in the Garden, You made clothes for them. Your love covers me. Your promise goes before me.

SO SHALL YOUR
DESCENDANTS BE

Abram was a wealthy man, but he had no son. What he did have, though, was a wonderful relationship with God. God had spoken throughout Abram's life, and Abram had listened. Each time Abram had an encounter with God and was given a promise, he built an altar, a place of remembrance. Abram grew to be an old man, and he had been hearing promises about his descendants for years. But Sarai was still barren.

I can imagine him thinking to himself, *Okay, I've had all of these promises about the land my future generations are going to inhabit and how my descendants will number like the sand, but I don't even have one child! Has God been talking about my legacy being left to some distant relative this whole time?*

But God knew what his heart was asking.

And He took him outside and said, "Now look toward the heavens, and count the stars, if you are able to count them." And He said to him, "So shall your descendants be." Then he believed in the Lord; and He reckoned it to him as righteousness (Genesis 15:5-6 NASB).

This is the kindness of the Lord. Abram needed reassurance on a promise from God that he had held close to his heart. God didn't turn His back on Abram or rebuke him for not having more faith. Instead, God just spoke to him. And, when Abram believed again, God gave Abram points for righteousness.

After that, Abram pushes for even more reassurance: *"He said, 'O Lord God, how may I know that I will possess it?'"* (Gen. 15:8 NASB). In response, God cuts a covenant with Abram. He tells him about the future of his descendants, how they would be enslaved, but that they would return to inhabit the land. He instructs Abram to bring the animal sacrifice and cut it up. God's goal is always connection. There are so many ways He could have handled Abram's insecurity and so many ways that he could have reiterated the promise, but God chooses to cut a covenant with His friend, Abram, in a way that speaks to Abram's heart.

Normally, both parties involved in the covenant would walk through the cut sacrifice, but this was a God-initiated promise to Abram. God passed through on His own, putting the weight of the covenant behind His words. Abram would have a child, he would leave a legacy, and God would care for his descendants. Whether they accessed the fullness of His blessing by following God's way or not was their choice, but His part of the promise would stand. Soon after this covenant was cut, Isaac was born, and God changed Abram's name to Abraham.

I carry promises over my life that have yet to be fulfilled. Sometimes the waiting feels unbearable, God, but I will not forget Your faithfulness. Help me to be like Abraham. Help me to be confident enough in our connection that I can bring You my honest questions and fears. Help me to be wise enough to leave those questions and fears in Your capable hands.

ABRAHAM'S PROMISE

J esus Christ shed His blood to cut a New Covenant with His creation. To forever bridge the divide of sin that had put a chasm between man and God, He initiated a New Covenant that was prophesied by Jeremiah.

> *"Behold, days are coming," declares the Lord, "when I will make a new covenant with the house of Israel and with the house of Judah…I will put My law within them and on their heart I will write it; and I will be their God, and they shall be My people"* (Jeremiah 31:31-33 NASB).

This New Covenant at once echoed and fulfilled the promises made to Abram. Instead of coming to earth as smoke and fire, God sent His Son to come to earth in human flesh to walk with us. Instead of a sacrificial animal, torn into two to signify the covenant, God offered His own Son—the spotless Lamb—whose body would be broken as the greatest sacrifice.

We are Abraham's promise fulfilled. Scripture says that, through our faith, we have become Abraham's descendants—as numerous as the stars in the sky and blessed by the Lord. *"And if you belong to Christ [are in Him Who is Abraham's Seed], then you are Abraham's offspring and [spiritual] heirs according to promise*" (Gal. 3:29 AMPC). We are "*heirs according to promise.*" We are the ones God was telling him about thousands of years ago, the ones who would inherit the promises and blessings of the Lord. We are the ones for whom God is a shield and a great rewarder (see Gen. 15:1). The Lord changed Abram's name to Abraham, the father of a multitude, but He also changed our names:

> *No longer do I call you slaves, for the slave does not know what His master is doing; but I have called you friends, for all things that I have heard from My Father I have made known to you* (John 15:15 NASB).

We have access to God in a way that Abraham, the man who was called the friend of God, had only dreamed about.

It's hard for me to even wrap my mind around what You sacrificed to save me, Papa, but I am so grateful. I will consciously choose to remember what Jesus did for me on that cross. Thank You for loving me and choosing me even when I didn't deserve it. Thank You for making a way for me to draw close to You every minute of every day.

NO GOING BACK

After Jesus' blood was spilled for the New Covenant, we became not only heirs of Abraham, but also co-heirs with Christ. We share in the inheritance of Jesus.

So then let no one boast in men. For all things belong to you, whether Paul or Apollos or Cephas or the world or life or death or things present or things to come; all things belong to you, and you belong to Christ; and Christ belongs to God (1 Corinthians 3:21-23 NASB).

What Jesus did for all of mankind on the cross was unconditional. He will never go back or change His mind. Accessing the fullness of the blessing of this covenant, though, is our choice entirely. When we take Communion, we are reminding ourselves of His sacrifice and the personal, unprecedented ways this New Covenant affects every area of our lives. *"He took the cup after they had eaten, saying, 'This cup which is poured out for you is the new covenant in My blood'"* (Luke 22:20 NASB). The blood that was shed was a covenant promise for all of eternity.

Nothing would be the same. The blood of Jesus paid for everything. It washed us white as snow, so we could enter the presence of the Lord without an intermediary and without fear. The blood of Jesus gave us freedom and authority. Hell has been defeated for all eternity. And now we get to boldly release Heaven on earth.

Thank You, Jesus, that You are not fickle or inconsistent. You are steadfast, and what You did on the cross for me is eternal. Will You show me one area of my life where I am living with restricted thinking that is not of You? I want to fully understand what it means that "all things belong to me." Open my eyes, Lord. Open my heart to Your revelation.

HEIRS WITH CHRIST

O nce, I went out to my son's property to walk and take Communion. They live out on 15 acres, so it's a peaceful place to think and pray. While I was meditating on Communion and all that Jesus went through on the cross, a thought popped into my head: "Every time you take Communion, you remind the devil of his failure."

There is power in the victorious blood of Jesus. That power was not just for the salvation of our souls at Calvary; that power is for right now. Romans says that *"the Spirit of life in Christ Jesus has set you free from the law of sin and of death"* (Rom. 8:2 NASB). The blood of Jesus wiped out the power of sin and the judgment that leads to death. Forever. God took back dominion over the earth and kicked out everything that was once ruled by darkness.

As heirs with Christ, we have that same authority through Jesus. And when I take Communion, I am not only aligning myself back up with my true identity as a daughter of God, I am also reminding the devil that he lost. The devil has to watch as I celebrate the resurrection power of Jesus.

The New Covenant has been cut, once and forever. Never again would the priest have to go into the Holy of Holies, not sure if he would come out alive, in order to rectify the sins of the people for another year. There was a shift in the atmosphere with the death and resurrection of Jesus Christ. It changed everything forever. We take his blood, represented in the wine, as a beautiful memorial of what Jesus did. By His blood, we can be saved, healed, and delivered.

My life testifies of Your goodness, God. Your provision surrounds me, Your comfort and love heal my heart, Your strength protects me, and Your beauty astonishes me. Let my life be a loud witness of Your lordship on the earth. Sin, darkness, shame, and death have been defeated. Let Your glory shine from every area of my life.

MIRACLE-WORKING GOD

In 2015, Bill started getting sick. For months, he had trouble eating and keeping food down. He would have a bad spell, and then his symptoms would seem to disappear for a little while. But then he'd get sick again. He tried changing his diet and getting medical advice, but it wasn't getting better. Finally, in the spring of 2016, while he was teaching in Europe, he became very ill. After speaking one evening, he went back to his hotel room and threw up 20 times. He was able to fly home, and once he got back we knew we needed some serious help.

We went to our local doctors in Redding, but they sent us to a specialist in San Francisco. By this time, Bill wasn't able to eat or drink anything. The hospital put him on an IV to keep him hydrated, and they ran a barrage of tests. Finally, they discovered that there was a growth in his small intestine that was almost completely blocking the passageway. His body was filling up with fluid. The medical staff prepared for surgery to remove the growth, not knowing how invasive of a procedure they would have to do.

Before we went down to San Francisco, we'd begun to take Communion every day at home. We would take the elements, give thanks, and proclaim all that Jesus did on the cross. We would declare, "This is Your body, broken for us. This is Your blood that was poured out for us. You died for our sins as well as our sicknesses. We align ourselves—spirit, soul, and body—with all that You did." Bill felt sick, but we were fighting it. And our weapon was Communion.

Once he was in the hospital in San Francisco, he wasn't able to take Communion anymore. He couldn't eat or drink anything at that point. So we said, "The circumstances don't matter; this hospital bed doesn't change a thing. We believe that God is our healer, and we're aligning ourselves with that every single day." I began to take Communion for him. We would pray together. I would take the elements for myself and for Bill. It was an incredibly sweet time of God's presence.

As the surgery day drew near, the doctors told us that unless the mass moved one centimeter from where it was positioned, they would need to perform a very serious, life-altering procedure. Hearing that, I immediately got the word out to family, friends, and intercessors, asking them to pray and take Communion for this shift. We needed that growth to move! The day of the procedure came, and the whole family waited, praying, to hear the news. When the surgeons were done, they gave us the update: the growth had shifted just enough. They were able to perform a procedure that was much less invasive with a quicker healing time. What could have been a scary day became a day of celebration. The whole family was cheering. We knew that God had done a miracle.

Thank You, Father, that You care about every aspect of our lives. Thank You that in Your presence is healing and complete restoration. I come to You today, laying down my pain, my anxiety, and the cries of my heart at Your feet. I trust You. I believe in You. Miracles are normal with You. Invade my life, today, with Your presence and power.

JEHOVAH RAPHA

Jesus died for our sins and for our sicknesses—anything that threatens to steal, kill, or destroy our life in Him is not of Him. When He went to the cross, He carried with Him every dark thing of the enemy and was the eternal sacrifice on our behalf. Isaiah 53:4-5 (NKJV) says:

> *Surely He has borne our griefs*
> *And carried our sorrows;*
> *Yet we esteemed Him stricken,*
> *Smitten by God, and afflicted.*
> *But He was wounded for our transgressions,*
> *He was bruised for our iniquities;*
> *The chastisement for our peace was upon Him,*
> *And by His stripes we are healed.*

This passage of Scripture prophesies the crucifixion and the only moment that God had to turn His face from Jesus. When Jesus took the weight of sin upon Himself, there was no way for God to be a part of that. Can you imagine the sorrow that Christ would have experienced? He had known what it was like to live in total union with the Father. I imagine that it would have been crushing for Him to be without God's presence.

Isaiah 53: 3, directly prior to the passage above, describes Jesus' rejection by humanity, saying that He was "*A Man of sorrows and acquainted with grief*" (NKJV). That word *grief* is the Hebrew word *choliy*, meaning sickness, disease, or sadness. It comes from a root word that literally means "to be worn down." Jesus carried all of our sorrows, our anxieties, our illnesses to the cross and died. He took the *choliy* of the world onto His shoulders so that we could be *sozo*—healed in spirit, soul, and body.

I know that there are some who believe that God no longer heals, that all miracles ended with the apostles. This is such a sad thought to me. Jesus endured the unimaginable on the cross in order that we could access salvation and wholeness. We deny the power of the cross when we deny the power of God healing today.

When we take Communion, remembering what Jesus accomplished on the cross, we are repeating the ultimate testimony again and again. Jesus Christ died so that we could be free of sin, sickness, and sorrow. He is the Healer, and He wants to do it again. Today. Communion has been underutilized far too often. It is a powerful tool, not only for intercession but also for healing. Take Communion, take it often, and apply the healing power of Jesus to your bodies!

Thank You, Father, that You care deeply about our bodies. We are not merely spirits chained to a fleshly form. You sent Your Son to earth, embodied, to show us how You would have us live. Your will is that we would be free from all forms of sorrow and sickness. I align my body with Heaven, in the name of Jesus, and embrace the healing that has already been paid for at the cross.

THE BREAD OF LIFE

John recounts that Jesus, speaking with the disciples, said, "*I am the bread of life; he who comes to Me will not hunger, and he who believes in Me will never thirst*" (John 6:35 NASB). When Jesus gives the disciples this imagery as a way for them to think about Him, He does something that He does often throughout the Gospels. He is taking a natural reality that they would be very familiar with and using that to explain a Kingdom truth. Our food pyramid has undergone some dramatic shifts recently, but for many cultures bread is a staple food in the normal diet. Jesus came from the throne room of Heaven. He is the King of all kings. But He doesn't say, "I am the caviar at your dinner party" or "I am the filet mignon of your life," or even "I am like mint chocolate chip ice cream!"

Instead, He says, "*I am the bread of life.*" Bread would have been foundational to the culture at the time. By equating Himself to bread, Jesus relates Himself to something familiar, but not trivial. Bread was intertwined with daily survival. Earlier in that same chapter, Jesus had fed 5,000 from a few loaves and fishes. The disciples had just witnessed the value of bread for the survival of a whole crowd.

Bread is life-sustaining. Of the 44 nutrients and vitamins necessary for human life found in food, bread made from freshly ground grain has 40. Unfortunately for all of us, mint chocolate chip ice cream doesn't hold the same nutritional value. When Jesus shares a meal with His disciples on that last Passover, He again offers Himself to His disciples as bread. Jesus breaks the bread, saying, "*this is My body*" (Mark 14:22). He offers us the chance to align our bodies with His body, broken and resurrected for us. He is our "*bread of life.*" Our survival depends on Jesus. He is life, hope, and healing.

You are my daily sustenance, Jesus. Your Spirit sustains and nourishes me. I need Your presence daily. Thank You that You have made Yourself accessible to me. Thank You that You are always there, closer than my very breath, when I turn to find You. You are my life, my hope, my healing, my home.

ALIGNING OURSELVES
WITH HIM

We never want to fall into the trap of thinking that Communion is some sort of golden ticket. Our relationship with God is not transactional, it is relational. Always. My desire is that you would see the power of remembering what He's done for us, of proclaiming who He is to us, and of aligning ourselves—spirit, soul, and body—with His presence.

Communion is not just a nice tradition. It represents the body and blood of Jesus Christ. We have access to the transformative power and grace of our Savior. Communion is a powerful tool at our disposal.

We get to come to the Lord with our *choliy*—our grief, our sickness, our pain—and make an exchange. Because of all that Christ did on the cross, we now have access to the same health and wholeness that is found in Him. Our God is the healer. It's not something that He chooses to do or not do; it is who He is.

When you take Communion, align yourself up with this reality. Plead the blood of Jesus over your soul, your spirit, and your body. And receive His transformative, healing presence into every area of your life.

Father, please forgive me for any way that I've made our precious relationship a transactional one. You are the healer, You are my provider, You are my strength and my protector. You are the Lord over every area of my life. I want to align every part of myself—spirit, soul, and body—with You.

THE BATTLE FOR TIME

As soon as I wake up, there are a thousand things competing for my attention. Before my feet hit the ground, I can read news from all over the world, find a recipe for dinner, scroll through photos on Instagram, listen to a worship song, and text my friend. And that's all in a matter of minutes! If the mind is a battlefield, then a big part of the current battle is a fight for space. It's a battle for time, for quiet, and for focus.

Now, I'm not saying that everyone needs to have hours each day set aside for time with the Lord. That's wonderful if you can do that, but not every season of life is conducive to that kind of time. When I was a young mother, that just wasn't possible. I had to learn how to turn my heart toward Him for a few minutes while doing the dishes or putting the baby to bed. What we can all do, though, is to create a meditative space—a space for remembering—during our time of Communion with God.

There are some days when, because of my schedule, I take Communion quickly. But most days I love to take the time to meditate on who God is and what He's done. The Lord wants to reveal different aspects of Himself to us, so every time I take Communion, I ask Him, "What does this mean today? What aspect of You do I need to have at the forefront of my mind today in order to keep myself aligned with You?" He is my daily bread. As I connect with Him, I meditate on His goodness and all that He's done. I take the time to remember.

When Jesus walked the disciples through the first Communion, He commanded them to remember. After both breaking the bread and taking the cup of wine, Jesus says, "*Do this in remembrance of Me*" (1 Cor. 11:24). God doesn't need to remember; He lives outside of time. Forgetfulness isn't something He deals with. Remembering is for us. We seem to forget something as soon as we turn around. Have you read the Old Testament? Part of me wants to shake my head every time I read of the Israelites forgetting the miraculous way God showed up for them two paragraphs prior, but then I think about my own life and how important remembering Him has been for me.

Holy Spirit, help me to see the moments throughout my day when I could turn my affection toward You, even for just a moment. I want to live out my value for You through the way I manage my time. Help me to remember Your goodness and Your kindness. Help me to recall all of the ways You have shown Your faithfulness to me.

REMEMBERING WHO HE IS

Memories have a powerful effect on our attitude and outlook. Bill teaches that if you are having a conflict with a friend, you should only share that conflict with someone who has genuine love for that person. Why? You don't want to vent to someone who will encourage division in the relationship. At that moment, you need someone who is able to remind you—in the midst of the pain—what you love about that person and the value of the relationship. You want someone who can help you pull out of any confusion or defensiveness and into the greater reality of love.

There's a similar motivation involved in weddings. Other than the joy of celebrating with loved ones, we invite our closest friends and family to witness our covenant because, when things get hard, we need those individuals to remind us who we are and what we've promised. Remembrance is vital for our walk as Christians. It keeps us aligned with the reality of who we are and the covenant that was made for us.

I've had many beautiful moments with the Lord throughout my life, but there are a few that I return to more often than others because of how they reorient my heart. One of these moments is our trip to Nome, Alaska. I went with a team of women up to northern Alaska to pray over our nation. It was the very first prophetic prayer act that I did out in the community, so I wasn't entirely sure how it was going to work out, but while we were on the trip, it became obvious that every single aspect—where we prayed, what we prayed, the people we met, the timing of our departure—had been orchestrated by God.

The time of prayer was powerful, but seeing His attention to detail and feeling so in sync with Him transformed me. I think back on this moment, and it reminds me not only of His faithfulness, but also how alive I feel when I'm connected to the Lord's heart in intercession. It's what I was made to do. I keep those memories close as powerful reminders to myself.

There are so many ways that I've experienced Your attentive, passionate love for me, God. Those moments are so precious to me, but so easy to forget. Holy Spirit, will You bring to mind some of the ways that Your love and power have intervened in my life? I will sit quietly in Your presence and wait to remember.

THE POWER OF MEMORY

Throughout the Bible, the Lord speaks to His people about the power of memory. In Deuteronomy, the Israelites are about to enter into the Promised Land. They've wandered the desert for 40 years, being sustained and guided supernaturally the whole way. Almost an entire generation has passed away, and the children of those who fled from Egypt are about to walk into the *"land flowing with milk and honey"* (Deut. 11:9 NKJV).

But first, Moses gives them some instructions from the Lord. In the first verse, he repeats the commandment, *"You shall therefore love the Lord your God, and always keep His charge, His statues, His ordinances, and His commandments"* (Deut. 11:1 NASB). But then he qualifies this commandment.

Moses says that the people who have seen the miracles of the Lord, the ones who lived through the parting of the Red Sea and the provision of manna, are the ones with the responsibility.

I am not speaking with your sons who have not known and who have not seen the discipline of the Lord your

God—His greatness, His mighty hand and His out-
stretched arm, and His signs and His works which He
did (Deut eronomy 11:2-3 NASB).

Moses is charging the ones who have seen the nature of
God firsthand with the commandments to love and obey
God. The testimony of their lives carries a responsibility,
not only for themselves but for the future generations.

*You have done so much for me, Lord, but sometimes
it's so easy for me to forget that in a moment of crisis. Father, would You give me a specific strategy for
keeping the moments of Your miraculous intervention in front of me at all times? I want to remember
all that You have done in my life so that I remember
how close You are to every moment of my life.*

INHABITING HIS PROMISE

Before entering the Promised Land, Moses tells the Israelites to remember their testimonies with the goodness of God: "*You shall teach them to your sons, talking of them when you sit in your house and when you walk along the road and when you lie down and when you rise up*" (Deut. 11:19 NASB). "Do not forget who the Lord is, and who He has been to you," Moses says.

Why is this so important? I can imagine Moses trying to get through to them, "Guys, please, no more of this idol business. Remember who God is and whose you are. Tell your children. Talk about it all of the time. Use any memory tool that will help you. Write it on your forehead, if that helps!"

He follows this encouragement by explaining to them why this is so important:

> **So that** *your days and the days of your sons may be multiplied on the land which the Lord swore to your fathers to give them, as long as the heavens remain above the earth*" (Deut eronomy 11:21 NASB).

Remembering is the key to inhabiting the Promised Land. The Lord wants to pour out blessings on them. He wants to bring them into "*a land of hills and valleys,* [that] *drinks water from the rain of heaven*" (Deut. 11:11 NASB). But in order for them to actually possess this land—to receive this blessing—they need to align their minds with His.

When we take Communion "*in remembrance*" of what Jesus did on the cross, we are stewarding the greatest testimony in history. The Israelites escaped Egypt after ten supernatural plagues rained down on their captors. They walked through the Red Sea on dry land. They were led by pillars of cloud and fire. They were fed supernaturally, never got sick, and wore the same clothes for 40 years. Yet they didn't have Jesus. They didn't have the cross or the resurrection. They didn't have a Savior who took away the sins of the world.

Matthew 11:11 makes it clear the kind of gift we have received. "*Truly I say to you, among those born of women there has not arisen anyone greater than John the Baptist! Yet the one who is least in the kingdom of heaven is greater than he*" (NASB). John the Baptist knew Jesus as family, followed God faithfully, yet he was never born again. He didn't know life with the resurrected Christ living inside of him. You and I, we get that honor. We have that responsibility.

You want to pour out blessings on me, God. Thank You that remembering all that You've done actually prepares me to inhabit a place of even greater blessing. I want to steward every testimony from my own life as well as those that I hear from others. They all prophesy as to who You are and what You want to do again on the earth. Open my eyes, Lord. Fill my heart with expectancy!

SETTING OUR MINDS

Memory is a powerful tool. It shapes our present by creating expectation for repetition. The brain is literally creating pathways from your thought patterns. Some of the discussion of this began in the New Age movement, but now scientists who study the brain are confirming what the Bible says—w hat you allow your mind to dwell on shapes your expectations and, ultimately, your perception of the world.

The neurons in the brain strengthen and change with our thought patterns. The more you make certain connections, the more likely your brain will make that connection in the future. Some describe it similarly to the way a popular hiking trail gets worn down and widened. For example, if you're used to thinking the world is out to get you, that neuropathway will have a strong connection in your brain. Something might happen to you, and you think, "Well, there it goes again. I knew bad things happen to me."

But the grace of the Lord always makes room for transformation. You can change these neuropathways by what you set your mind on. So when Paul writes to the Colossians and advises them, "*Set your mind on the things above,* not on the things that are on earth. For you have died and your life is hidden with Christ in God" (Col. 3:2-3 NASB), it's not just a nice idea. It's actually advice that will change the "hardwiring" of our brains. We are new creations. We know a reality that is greater than any circumstance we can see. We have "the mind of Christ," and God is inviting us to use it (see 1 Cor. 2:16).

> Thank You for Your grace, God, as I learn and grow, adjusting some of the thought patterns I've gotten used to. Thank You that science confirms Your Word—m y mind is being transformed as I dwell on Your character and Your reality. Change is always possible with You. There is always hope; I am never stuck. I have the mind of Christ!

THE POWER OF TESTIMONY

At Bethel, sharing testimonies is a big part of our culture. We have a two-hour senior staff meeting each week in which we spend a large portion of the time sharing about what the Lord is doing all over the earth. It's amazing to hear about the miracles. The world is truly getting better all of the time. But when we hear those, we don't just stop with marveling at God's goodness. We also say, "Do it again, God!"

As Bill says, the power of the testimony never depreciates. Whenever you revisit a story of God's faithfulness or His divine disruption in your life, you are revisiting a place of divine encounter. Remembering what He's done in your life never loses power. God is the same yesterday, today, and tomorrow. So when you hear of a miracle that has happened in someone else's life, you know that God has just set the legal precedent of what He wants to continue. Testimonies are not just fond memories. They have a lifespan that's eternal. They continually give God praise.

We were designed to impact the world around us. We have been given the charge to represent a good God and infuse every situation with Heaven. We cannot do that, though, without feeding ourselves on all that God has done for us, thereby building our faith and our hope for what is to come.

A beautiful thread weaves between our past, our present, and our future. In our past, we have what God has done—all of the stories of His faithfulness and grace. In our present, we have the command to remember those testimonies, to build our trust in God and align ourselves with Him. From that place, change will come. *"For whenever you eat this bread and drink this cup, you proclaim the Lord's death until he comes"* (1 Cor. 11:26 NIV). The act of proclaiming is like sharing the testimony. It is releasing the reality of the cross into the world. When you're remembering God and trusting in Him completely, then you are filled with hope for the future of the world around you.

We can take Communion in remembrance of all that He has done for the world and for ourselves personally, and we can look toward the future with hope. Matthew 17:20 says, *"if you have faith the size of a mustard seed, you will say to this mountain, 'Move from here to there,' and it will move; and nothing will be impossible to you"* (NASB). This promise is embedded in the body and blood of Christ.

Holy Spirit, will You remind me of one story from the Bible that I can pull on during this season? I want to dwell on the eternal testimony of who You are and build my faith for the situation I am facing. You have done it before, and You will do it again. I will declare the truth of who You are and who I am to You over my situation, today!

MAINTAINING GRATITUDE

Often, we don't really want to remember the brutality of what Jesus went through for us. It's gruesome and uncomfortable. But when I remind myself of the details of Christ's death, I find that it keeps my heart in a posture of overwhelming gratitude. It also renews my perspective on whatever challenge I'm going through. For 33 years, Jesus had lived on earth—three of those spent serving in a fruitful, but probably exhausting, time of public ministry. As He neared the end of His life, Jesus wrestled with what He was about to do.

He knelt down and prayed, saying, "Father, if it is Your will, take this cup away from Me; nevertheless not My will, but Yours, be done." Then an angel appeared to Him from heaven, strengthening Him. And being in agony, He prayed more earnestly. Then His sweat became like great drops of blood falling down to the ground" (Luke 22:41-44 NKJV).

Jesus was the only one, besides the Father, who was aware of what He was about to go through. The intensity of that anticipation, not only of His own physical death, but also of the agony of being separated from the Father because of the sin of the world, must have been so painful that He literally sweat blood. When He was carrying that reality, the betrayal by Judas and the rejection from His closest disciples must have been an added weight on His heart.

When I take Communion, I stop and remember this betrayal. I don't just dwell on the injustice for its own sake, but I do want to remember the cost of what Jesus did so that I can truly value His gift to me. Thinking through all that He went through in the days leading up to His death also paints a picture to me of how to walk through pain. These moments in the life of Jesus are so brutal and yet so beautiful.

Jesus knew that Peter would deny Him, that His disciples would abandon Him, and that Judas was going to betray Him. But He still sat down to a meal with them and shared Communion. "*The Lord Jesus, on the night he was betrayed, took bread, and when he had given thanks, he broke it*" (1 Cor. 11:23-24 NIV). There are a few aspects here that teach me so much. He was well aware of the betrayal, yet Jesus still invited Judas to break bread with Him. He gave thanks. Jesus filled His heart with gratitude, despite being aware that He was about to die and the very people He was dying for were betraying Him. I can't imagine the strength that Jesus had to have to walk through that moment the way that He did. Knowing that He was going to be crucified, He gave thanks. In the midst of betrayal, He opened His heart to His disciples.

So when I'm remembering the betrayal of Jesus, I'm not just focusing on the injustice. I'm focusing on Jesus. I'm reminding myself of the way that He walked through betrayal. If Jesus can do that, then He's offering me a model for how to deal with my own hurts and grievances. He's showing me what His love can overcome.

I never want to forget the incredible price You paid for my freedom, Jesus. I never want to forget the agony You suffered or the despair You must have felt. I am overwhelmed with gratitude for who You are and all that You have done. Your choice to give thanks in the midst of betrayal is one I want to emulate in my own life.

HE STAYED

O ver the years, Bill and I have experienced a few people who have focused a lot of energy on attacking our lives and ministry. One day, when we were in the middle of praying for our friends and family, Bill started to pray for each of the people who had come against us. He began to pray a blessing over their families, praying for God's grace to be on their lives and for their physical health. I sat there listening to my husband and felt totally convicted. I remembered what Jesus went through, and something clicked in my spirit. I realized, "Oh my gosh, I can love these people. Despite everything that's going on, I can love them."

Jesus didn't shy away from the suffering involved in His sacrifice. The agony of anticipation He experienced in the Garden of Gethsemane and the betrayal by His disciples was followed by excruciating physical pain. He was forced to carry a heavy cross for miles while a crowd threw stones at Him and spit in His face. Once the cross was erected, long nails pierced through the tendons in His wrists and the bones in His feet. For three hours, our Jesus suffered the most horrifying pain as He hung on the cross, experiencing the weight of sin and the distance of the Father.

As a part of meditative Communion, I like to remind myself of what He went through on the cross. One day, I was imagining His suffering, and I realized, "He stayed up on that cross!" Jesus was fully God and fully man. He didn't have to do anything He didn't want to do. He could have taken Himself right off of that cross if He'd chosen to, but He stayed. He stayed for me. He stayed for us. That realization brought a whole new wave of gratitude, because I know that I couldn't have done that. I would have been saying, "Sorry, Dad, but I can't handle this!" Instead, He stayed.

There is a weight to remembering the cost that Jesus paid. I never want anyone to cultivate the heaviness that leads to depression. But there is an important humility and gravity that comes when you are remembering *how* His body was broken for us and *how* His blood was poured out for us. When I meditate on His experience, I remember all over again that His blood is sufficient for anything I am going through. Jesus paid the ultimate sacrifice so that I could be free and whole. If something is threatening that, I know it's not of the Lord. I can see what He went through to untangle me forever from sin and sickness.

Thank You, Jesus, that I don't have to muster up the ability from within myself to love my enemies. You commanded it, so Your grace empowers me to obey. I open my heart up wide to You today, Lord. Show me any area of pain, betrayal, or disappointment that I'm trying to carry in my own strength. I am so grateful that You stayed up on the cross for me and for everyone who has done me wrong. Help me to fully comprehend the power of Your blood.

MEMORY, TRUST, OBEDIENCE

Psalm 78 catalogues the faithfulness of God to the Israelites. Unlike most of the psalms, this one reads like a history lesson, but embedded within the narrative is a warning: Do not *"forget the works of God"* (Ps. 78: 7 NKJV).

We will not conceal them from their children,
But tell to the generation to come the praises of the
Lord,
And His strength and His wondrous works that He has
done.
For He established a testimony in Jacob
And appointed a law in Israel,
Which He commanded our fathers
That they should teach them to their children,
That the generation to come might know, even the
children yet to be born,
That they may arise and tell them to their children,
That they should put their confidence in God
And not forget the works of God,
But keep His commandments,
And not be like their fathers,
A stubborn and rebellious generation,

A generation that did not prepare its heart
And whose spirit was not faithful to God
(Psalm 78:4-8 NASB).

The psalmist goes on to explain about the "*stubborn and rebellious generation*" (vs. 8), detailing the many times that they turned from the Lord and just how poorly that worked out for them each time. Through the mistakes of the Israelites, the author gives us a glimpse of what is at stake if we choose not to actively remember. Verse 7 makes the connection between memory, trust, and obedience: "*That they should put their confidence in God and not forget the works of God, but keep His commandments*" (NASB). Dwelling on the goodness of God, continually reminding ourselves of His faithfulness and His promises—these are the building blocks of trust. And when we trust God, aligning ourselves with His commandments comes so much more naturally. Without our keeping Him in the forefront of our minds, that confidence crumbles, and fear takes hold.

I love how *The Passion Translation* puts it in verse 22, talking about the Israelites who forgot God: "*They turned away from faith and walked away in fear; they failed to trust in his power to help them when he was near.*" There are very real consequences to our forgetting who God is. When His goodness and faithfulness are not fresh in our mind, we can become calloused toward God. We can feel hesitant to trust in His goodness. And that can lead to a heart that has not been cultivating gratitude. We can see the results of that within our own lives and the lives of the Israelites. As soon as they started forgetting, they began to fear, and they put their trust in something else. Later, the same psalm speaks of the Lord's reaction to their unfaithfulness. *"He abandoned the dwelling place at Shiloh... and gave up His strength to captivity and His glory into the hand of the adversary"* (Ps. 78:60-61 NASB). This verse is incredibly sobering. Because of the Israelites' forgetfulness, because they turned from trusting in God completely, He allowed His presence to be removed from their midst. They were no longer recipients of His strength, and they no longer had access to His glory.

Father, will You show me any area of my life where I am not completely trusting in You? Will You bring to mind every part of my thinking that has been ruled by fear? I want to immerse myself in the testimonies of Your goodness. I want to build up my trust in You. I want to surrender my heart in full obedience.

HIS BLOOD IS ENOUGH

We live under the New Covenant. God has promised never to remove His presence from us, but we still have the same choice that the Israelites had. Will we remember and trust in God's love for us, or will we turn to fear and fending for ourselves?

The psalmist describes an all-too-familiar heart issue: *"Even when they saw God's marvels, they refused to believe God could care for them"* (Ps. 78:32 TPT). Will He take care of me? Will He provide for me? Was His blood enough for what I'm going through? Each time we take Communion, we are testifying to the enormous, radical love of God. We are reminding ourselves that we had a debt that we could never, ever repay and that we were condemned to death; there was nothing we could do about it.

But God. His love was so extravagant that He sent His Son to die in our place, to suffer indescribable pain so that He could take on the sins of the world. *"For God so loved the world, that He gave His only begotten Son, that whoever believes in Him shall not perish, but have eternal life"* (John 3:16 NASB). This was the first verse I learned as a child. It's a powerful one that we can take for granted because it's so familiar. I would encourage you, as you take Communion, to meditate on this verse. Allow your remembrance of Him to take you to a new level of understanding. It was all for love. Love took Him to that cross, and love kept Him there. When you take Communion, experience the invitation to remember the weighty reality of His absolute and perfect love for you.

Jesus, forgive me for those moments when I've doubted Your faithfulness, Your goodness, or the power of Your blood. I know that You will take care of me. Your provision is more than enough for my life. Your blood covers me in every situation I face. As I take communion today, I will meditate on the immensity of Your unearned, perfect love for me.

TOOLS OF INTERCESSION

I was born to pray. When I go up to the high places—a mountaintop or the top of a city building—to pray and worship, I feel as though I'm doing what I was born to do. I'm in my element. I often go with a team of friends to various places to intercede, and in the last few years we've added Communion to the arsenal of tools we use during these times.

Too often Communion can get locked into the routine of church culture. There are great, logistical reasons for churches to have Communion once per month. But that doesn't mean we have to limit ourselves to that! Like every other aspect of our walk with God, if we are only experiencing Communion within the four walls of the church, we are missing out on a gift from Jesus.

Communion is a powerful tool of intercession. And because of that, it's applicable in every area of our lives. At the end of 2017, Bethel invited people to prayer walk in their neighborhoods for three months. In that time, people traveled alone or with friends to whatever part of the city they had on their hearts. We offered a list of prayer targets, but those walking were encouraged to pray, take Communion, and declare truth over our city and our nation. One of the ways that we can tap into the transformative power of Communion is by taking it into our communities. These walks are a chance for us to take ownership over our land and the atmospheres over our cities.

You love my personality, Jesus. You know what makes me come alive! Thank You that my prayer time never needs to be scripted or stiff. I can be fully myself with You, because You love exactly how You made me. Holy Spirit, open my mind to tools for intercession that I could use as a part of my prayer time. Help me break out of any box I've put myself in when it comes to spending time with You!

PREACHING THE GOOD NEWS

First Corinthians 11 says that, when we participate in Communion, we are proclaiming the Lord's death. *"For as often as you eat this bread and drink the cup, you proclaim the Lord's death until He comes"* (1 Cor. 11:26 NASB). On the surface, that verse sounds like we're just reminding everyone that Jesus died. But it's more than that. That phrase *"you proclaim"* is the Greek word *kataggello.* It's the same word, used throughout the New Testament, that is also translated as "preached." *"And when they arrived in Salamis, they* **preached** *the word of God in the synagogues of the Jews"* (Acts 13:5 NKJV).

When you take Communion, you're telling the world about the Lord's death. Every time you partake in the body and blood of Jesus Christ, you are preaching the Gospel. How? Communion is most often thought of as a time of quiet reflection, not bold proclamation. Yet that word *kataggello* is undeniably assertive.

Each time you take Communion, you align yourself with the broken body and the shed blood of Christ. You are remembering what He's done for you. But you are also aligning yourself with what happened three days later. When we are lined up with the reality of Christ—in spirit, soul, and body—we release that reality into the world. We preach the Good News, not just from a pulpit or with our voices; we preach the Good News with who we are. We show the goodness of God with how we handle situations in our businesses and in our families. Every time we take Communion, then, we are reminding ourselves that we are Christians—little Christs. When we remind ourselves who we are, we can reveal to the world who He is.

When we remember who He is and who we are, we can offer the world a glimpse of a God they may have never seen before. We can reveal to them a Father who cares, who desires to be intricately involved in every aspect of their lives.

The Lord wants to invade every area of your life. He is not only interested in being with you in Heaven; He wants Heaven to invade earth in your families, in your businesses, and in your communities. The Bible says that He knows "*the very hairs of your head*" (Luke 12:7 NKJV). He knows what is in our hearts, and He cares about what we care about.

I want to share the Good News of Jesus Christ, raised from the dead, with every aspect of my life. Holy Spirit, fill me with Your presence so that the way I do my job declares Your goodness. Give me wisdom for my family so that the way we love one another shows the world Your covenant devotion to us. Heal every area of my life, Lord, so that I might reveal Your nature to the world.

RELEASE THE TESTIMONIES

Many years ago, we had a strange experience where a roadrunner kept coming to our prayer meetings. For months, this bird would show up outside of the building when we would gather to worship. We had no idea what was going on, but it felt significant.

One night, the bird snuck in the building while one of our custodial team was cleaning. Every time the custodian would stop working to put on some worship music, the bird would stop and watch. Every time the young man would move, the bird would follow him. After a while of this, a door opened from another room and spooked the bird. It ran down the hallway into the plate-glass window and died.

The whole story was too strange, so Bill went to the Lord and just asked Him what was going on with this bird. Very clearly, he heard, "What I'm bringing into the House had better have a way of being released from the House or it will die in the House."

The Spirit of God lives inside every believer and will never leave. But we have the honor of stewarding His presence. God has given the gift of His body and blood to

His Church. But I want to encourage you to release the power of Communion from the four walls of the church and into your family, your business, your community, etc. There is no area of your life that Communion with God cannot improve.

The Bible says that "*the testimony of Jesus is the spirit of prophecy*" (Rev. 19:10 NKJV). Whatever God has done before, He wants to do again. Grab ahold of them. Let your faith rise. Align yourself with the resurrected Christ. And witness the wonder-working power of Jesus.

Forgive me, Lord, for the things of You that I've kept for myself out of fear or a desire to remain comfortable. Help me know how to release the love, peace, and power that You've poured into my life. I want to be a river of Your presence—constantly receiving from You, constantly pouring out to others. Open my eyes to Your miraculous inter-ventions. Open my heart to opportunities to share Your presence with the world.

A SOBER OCCASION

J esus never requires perfection in order to come to Him. That is the scandal of His saving grace. We don't need to be anxious about taking Communion, searching for any potential hidden sin. Fear is never productive; it just gets in the way of love's transforming power. However, when we participate in the body and blood of Christ, we do want to posture our hearts in an intentional way. This intentionality not only brings the respect and honor due to the sacrament, but it also helps us to create the space in our hearts for the Spirit of God to move and transform us through Communion.

Often, when we focus so much on what divides us, we can miss out on honoring some valuable aspects of different Christian traditions. Even though I love our free-flowing worship, there is something so beautiful about a formal liturgy. Similarly, I think we can learn from the way the Catholic Church honors Communion, teaching the children what it means and making a special event of their first occasion. When we participate in Communion, it is important for there to be a sense of soberness. I don't mean *somber*, as in "gloomy or depressing." Far from it.

But there needs to be a sense of gravity about what we are getting to participate in.

We have such a good Father, who is so incredibly full of grace, but I would never want to lose sight of His holiness or His awesome power. On the one hand, we have Jesus inviting the little children to come to Him. And on the other, we have Jesus returning to earth with eyes that flame like fire. It's not either/or; it's both/and. When we participate in the body and blood of Jesus Christ, sober reverence is a healthy and appropriate reaction.

Thank You, God, that You don't want my relationship with You to be filled with fear and anxiety. You are holy and awesome, and You are kind and gentle. Thank You that You have made it easy for me to come into Your presence. But I never want to treat Your presence casually. I never want to forget the sacrifice You made to save me.

IN EVERYTHING
GIVE THANKS

T he Bible tells us to *"Rejoice always; pray without ceasing; in everything give thanks; for this is God's will for you in Christ Jesus"* (1 Thess. 5:16-18 NASB). I often hear people yearning to know God's will for their lives, but it says it right here. Stay thankful. Stay connected to God. When the Bible tells us to be thankful no matter the circumstance, it is not expecting us to create an emotion out of thin air. Gratitude is a response. There has to be a previous action or reality. When we take Communion, we are responding to all that the Lord has done and continues to do for us. Keeping our hearts postured toward the Lord in gratitude is one of the biggest keys to success we find throughout the Bible.

Hebrews 13:15 encourages us to *"continually offer up a sacrifice of praise to God"* (NASB). We've all been in the midst of experiences in which the phrase *"sacrifice of praise"* feels very real. When you're exhausted or hurting, sometimes worship and expressing gratitude is the last thing you want to do. But look at the Samaritan leper. Ten leprous men were healed by Jesus, but only one of them fell down to give Him thanks. Jesus wasn't in need of gratitude, but He knew that it would do something for the man. Jesus asked about the other nine men who hadn't returned, and then He told the Samaritan, "*Stand up and go; your faith has made you well*" (Luke 17:19 NASB). The man was already healed. But that word *well* is that Hebrew word *sozo* again. His body had been healed, but there was something about his expression of gratitude that made him whole.

Psalm 50 says that "*He who offers a sacrifice of thanksgiving honors Me; and to him who orders his way aright I shall show the salvation of God*" (Ps. 50:23 NASB). This is such a powerful verse. We have been made "*a royal priesthood*" (1 Pet. 2:9 NASB). As believers under the New Covenant, we now have the privilege of ministering to the Lord. When we offer up a "*sacrifice of praise,*" we are bringing honor to God. Focusing our hearts on gratitude brings Him glory, which alone is enough. But the Bible goes on to explain that gratitude also reorients us correctly, inviting the "*salvation of God*" into our lives. That word *salvation* is the Hebrew word *yesha*, which means "rescue and safety," but it also means "deliverance, prosperity, and victory." The psalmist said to "*enter His gates with thanksgiving and His courts with praise*" (Ps. 100:4 NASB). When we come to the Lord with thankfulness, we have access to His presence and His covering. We get to participate in His victory.

Holy Spirit, would You help me to think of ten things that I'm thankful for in this season? I want to dwell on Your goodness, God. I want to remind myself of all of the ways You have been my faithful Father, even in challenging seasons. I will offer up a sacrifice of praise to You, because You are so worthy of it all.

THE BODY OF CHRIST

I love the story of the first miracle that Jesus did. I love that Mary pulled Jesus' public ministry into the limelight before it was time. And I love that Jesus created wine for a party. Jesus loves celebration. The dictionary defines *celebration* as "the action of marking one's pleasure at an important event or occasion by engaging in enjoyable, typically social, activity." We can celebrate alone, of course, but more often a celebration is an experience we want to share with the people we love.

When we take Communion, it is our chance to celebrate with our brothers and sisters in Christ. Jesus has changed our lives, and that deserves a party. After all, what's a celebration without friends? There is something very special about corporate Communion—partaking of the body and blood of Christ with the vibrant, diverse body of Christ. Communion is a vertical realigning of ourselves with Christ, but it is also a horizontal realigning—w e are the body of Christ.

God loves unity. It was His idea. This is why examining our hearts is such an important part of Communion. Not because we have to prove to God that we're worthy of His blood and body. We already know that's impossible.

We examine our hearts because it's a time of reunion, both with the Spirit of God and with our fellow believers. In corporate Communion, we get to stand with others and confess that He took a burden from our shoulders that we could never carry. Experiencing that radical grace means that we now get to access and release that grace to others. We get to offer forgiveness to others, cleansing our hearts from the detrimental effects of bitterness and unforgiveness.

The individual relationship with God is crucial to our lives and foundational to our beliefs. We must have that time in the secret place. But the Lord also loves it when we gather, united, in His name. He promises that "*where two or three have gathered together in My name, I am there in their midst*" (Matt. 18:20 NASB).

Communion is a time of celebration. Like eating the wedding cake and toasting with champagne after the vows have been exchanged, Communion commemorates the covenant that has been made between our Creator and ourselves. This celebration also solidifies and reminds us of the union that we have with those around us. Jesus loves His Church. He is coming back for a strong, healthy, and united Bride.

Jesus, bring to mind anyone with whom I have division and disconnection. Help me to examine my own heart. Am I carrying any offense? Have I made a case against anyone? Where are the areas where my own pain has made me self-protective? Search my heart, Holy Spirit. I want to release anything that is not mine to carry so that I can celebrate freely with my brothers and sisters in Christ.

A GREATER REALITY

It's all about Him. Everything changes when we align ourselves with God. As Bill says, "The Holy Spirit wants to reveal Himself *to* you so that He can reveal Himself *through* you." We are citizens of Heaven, but we have an assignment to fulfill on earth—that is releasing the reality of Heaven into every situation, every relationship, and every corner of the earth. But how can we do that? Not through our own strength, surely. Scripture says that *"we have the mind of Christ"* (1 Cor. 2:16 NKJV). It says that we have died and have been raised with Jesus (see Rom. 6:4). It says that our old man has gone and we are a new creation (see 2 Cor. 5:17) and that Christ lives within us (see Gal. 2:20). The Bible is 100 percent true, so if I'm not experiencing those statements all of the time, then there must be a reality that is greater and *truer* than the one that I am experiencing.

That we would need reminding of this greater reality comes as no surprise to the Lord. It's like He sat us all down at that table with the disciples in that upper room and said, "Listen, I know. I know some days are going to be hard. I know there are going to be moments when it feels like the reality of Heaven is far away. Your child is sick or you lost your job or your best friend died or you did that thing you swore you would stop doing. I know. I'm leaving you something—My body and My blood— to remind you who you are and where your true home is. I'm leaving you this reminder of My salvation, My healing, the comfort of My presence, and My victorious return. Take it. Remember Me. Be everything I created you to be so that My Kingdom can invade every single one of those situations, and the world can know a good, good Father."

Human nature is constantly attempting to create rules outside of a relationship. Communion is not a magic pill, and God is not a vending machine. He does not want us to eat a wafer and drink some grape juice every day so that He will grant our wishes. Communion is about lining ourselves up with Him—spirit, soul, and body. It is a chance for us to remember the debt of sin that hung around our necks—too big for us to ever repay on our own—and the way that our Jesus took that debt with Him to the cross so that you and I could *"have life, and have it abundantly"* (John 10:10 NASB). It's a chance for us to come—in all humility and honor— into the presence of the Lord, to praise His name for all that He has done, and to celebrate in union with other believers. Take this tool, given to us by Jesus Himself, and use it frequently. You will not remain the same. That is His promise.

It's so easy to forget, Lord, that today's troubles are not my greatest reality. They can loom so large in my mind, clouding out my awareness of Your goodness. Forgive me, God. I know that isn't the truth. The truth is that I have the mind of Christ. I have died and have been raised again with Jesus. My old self has disappeared, and I am now a new creation. Christ lives in me, and I will release Heaven onto the earth!

PAST, PRESENT, FUTURE

We are taught in the Scriptures that in taking Communion we are *proclaiming the Lord's death until He comes* (see 1 Cor. 11:26). I like to picture *proclaiming* as a bold and confident shout! We are declaring in fullness the redemptive work of Jesus found in the Gospel. Every time we take the bread and the wine/juice in remembrance, it is a prophetic proclamation of what has already happened, as well as what is yet to come. Consider this— Communion declares that Jesus died for us and is returning for us.

When people surrender their life to Jesus, they are born again. In other words, they're saved. We know this teaching from God's Word. But then the Bible also says, "*Work out your own salvation with fear and trembling*" (Phil. 2:12). The implication is that I am also *being saved*. This doesn't deny what happened to me when I received Christ. It just emphasizes the daily ongoing process of personal transformation. So not only were you once saved, but you are also being saved right now.

The crowning touch to this glorious truth of our salvation comes when we die to meet Him or He returns to take us to Heaven. In this coming event, we find that we *will be* saved. Our salvation will then be complete. Participating in Communion is a wonderful privilege that declares what I call *the bookends of our salvation* in that it addresses the past and the future. Sharing in the broken body and the shed blood of Jesus helps us with the present.

Every time I take Communion, I am proclaiming the reality of my salvation and the power of the Gospel. Thank You, Jesus, that I have been saved by what You did on the cross. Thank You that, as I open my heart to You, aligning myself with Your perspective, I am becoming more and more like You every day. Thank You that I get to look forward to the complete salvation of Heaven.

GRATITUDE IN THE MIDST OF DIFFICULTY

The most complete passage on the rite of Communion in the Bible is found in First Corinthians 11. In it, Paul unwraps the insight given to him through an encounter with Jesus Himself. In verses 23 and 24, he says:

> For I received from the Lord that which I also delivered to you: that the Lord Jesus on the same night in which He was betrayed took bread; and when He had given thanks, He broke it and said, "Take, eat" (1 Corinthians 11:23-24 NKJV).

Please picture something powerful—the very night that Jesus was betrayed, He gave thanks. In the midst of the ultimate betrayal, He gave an offering of thanksgiving. He didn't just tell us to praise Him in hard times; He gave us the ultimate example to follow. In betrayal, He gave thanks.

Thankfulness is one of the most vital attributes within the reach of every person alive. If I could prayerfully lay hands on people and impart a thankful heart, without question, I would. And I would make that the single greatest focus of my life. An impartation of thankfulness would have the greatest impact on the hearts and minds of people. It would literally change the world as we know it. Thankful people attract breakthrough.

Following the major sporting events like the Super Bowl, World Series, World Cup, and the like, it has become common to see athletes thank God for enabling them to win. I love to see them boast in God and testify of Him every chance they get. But let's be honest— it's not that challenging to give thanks when you've won. The real prize is when we give Him thanks in the middle of something difficult or wrong. That's where the pearl is formed, so to speak. Pearls are formed through irritation. Whenever we give thanks in the middle of hard things, we are presenting something to Him that is priceless. Jesus did it at His darkest moment—betrayal.

Holy Spirit, I want to be known as a person with a thankful heart. Help me to practice expressing my gratitude when I wake up, before I sleep, and throughout my day. Open my eyes to Your grace upon my life. Empower me, during moments of heartache and betrayal, to follow Jesus' lead and offer up a grateful heart.

PAUSING TO REMEMBER

I n 1 Corinthians 11: 24 (NKJV), Jesus said of the bread, *"'Take, eat; this is My body which is broken for you.'"* Please listen to what He said. He said, *"This is My body."* There is an invitation into a kind of reverence with this statement: *"which is broken for you; do this in remembrance of Me."* Verse 25 continues: *"In the same manner He also took the cup after supper, saying, 'This cup is the new covenant in My blood. This do, as often as you drink it, in remembrance of Me.'"*

It's just like the Lord to give us things to do that position us to remember Him. Making this a ritual or tradition that has lost its meaning is so unnecessary. In our hearts, we all have the intention of serving the Lord fully and with complete abandonment. But if you're like me, you probably sometimes go for hours in a day without thinking of Him. We're living from His blessing, from His commission, but there are times in the day when we aren't abiding in that face-to-face privilege that we have with God. We are working faithfully, playing with the kids or taking care of our daily business. With no condemnation, we can all admit that life gets busy. But in His kindness, the Lord gives us tools that help us to bring Him back into our minds.

Pausing to remember is a principle established throughout Scripture. In the Old Testament, Israel miraculously crossed a river on dry ground. Once they did, they were instructed to put a pile of stones on the same side of the river they crossed over to. This way, every time they passed the place where the miraculous had occurred, the stones would trigger the memory. The goodness of the Lord was brought back to mind (see Josh. 4:1-24). The devil wants to control your memories. He wants to influence how you think about your past. He wants to influence your perspective on the reality that's going on around you. And he does so by keeping you focused on the things that were disappointing, or the areas of past failures, or where you were wronged. The Lord, on the other hand, constantly invites you to return to a redemptive focus where you concern yourself with what God is saying and what God is doing.

Thank You, Lord, for giving us tools that You knew we would need in order to keep our minds and hearts aligned with Yours. You knew that life would get busy. I want to grow in my intentional stewardship of the stories of Your goodness in my life. Would You give me another, practical tool for remembering Your promises for me and the supernatural interventions that I've experienced?

HEALING FOR TODAY

I saiah 53, the prophetic passage on healing, reads, *"Surely He has borne our griefs"* (Isaiah 53:4 NKJV). The literal word for "griefs" is *sicknesses.* In this passage, Isaiah is, in fact, saying, *"Surely He has borne our* [sicknesses] *and carried our sorrows; yet we esteemed him stricken, smitten by God, and afflicted."* When Jesus died on the cross, the Scripture says, "He became sin" (see 2 Cor. 5:21). And when He became sin and died in our place, the Father's anger and wrath were poured out on Him as He became the very thing that was working to destroy us. He took my place and bore what I deserved. Jesus asked the Father, "Why did You turn Your face from Me? Why did You forsake Me?" (See Matthew 27:46 and Psalm 22:1.) The Father forsook Him because Jesus became sin. He poured out His wrath upon His own Son, who had become what was destroying mankind.

Everybody knows you get a new body in Heaven. There's no sickness there, there's no weeping there, there's no pain, no conflict, no confusion. In Heaven, everything is wonderful. So it's important to see that this part of His provision is for now. *"By His stripes we are healed"* (Isa. 53:5 NKJV). Peter quoted the passage from Isaiah in this way: *"by whose stripes you were healed"* (1 Pet. 2:24 NKJV). Notice it is past tense. It has already been accomplished on our behalf.

The body of the broken Savior made a full and complete payment, not only for my healing, but for health—spirit, soul, and body. This is the provision of the Lord. And that's its purpose. Remembering Jesus' broken body in Communion is not just a nice sentimental moment when we give thanks that He died and we get to go to Heaven. It is all that, but a million times more. It's a divine moment.

Let's say somebody gives you a car. They've gone down to the dealership and paid in cash, and they say, "Just go on down there, give them this card, and they'll give you the car. Everything has been paid for—the taxes are paid, the tank is full of gas, and I've covered insurance for the first five years. Go, get your car!" It would be foolish for you to go down there and insist on paying for the car again. Yet many people are trying to pay for their healing that's already been purchased. It's a gift that we all qualify for.

By the stripes of Jesus, I was healed. You paid the price for my salvation—spirit, soul, and body—and I will receive Your healing presence today. Any ailment or pain in my body must leave. Every fear tormenting my soul, be gone. And anything not of the Kingdom of God must bow to the name of Jesus. I have been set free!

LET GOD ARISE

Communion is a weapon of war, and I really believe that. This meal is not only an act of celebration but also a military tool of battle. We may not feel like we are engaging in war, but there are many things that we do—celebrating His kindness and His goodness, delighting in His presence, and giving praise—that all have a military effect on the demonic realm. Psalm 68:1 says, *"Let God arise, let His enemies be scattered"* (NASB). When we exalt the Lord, there is an effect on the realms of darkness.

The Lord has given us basically four different weapons for spiritual warfare: the blood of Jesus (Communion), the Word of God, the name of Jesus, and praise. Those are the four basic weapons that we believers use in our life that defeat and overcome the assaults that the enemy brings against us. None of them are focused on the devil. All of them are focused on the provision of the Lord and the Person of the Lord Jesus Christ.

As a church, we're on a journey to learn how to access all that God has purchased for us. The blood of Jesus is the legal basis for all victory. The cross of Jesus was so thorough in its victory that everything you will ever need throughout eternity was purchased at this one event. There's no other event in history that was so all-inclusive. A hundred billion years from now we will still be feeding off of what was provided for in the sacrifice of this unblemished Lamb.

I know that my battles are not against other people, but rather against the powers and principalities of darkness. You have already won the victory, Jesus, so I advance into warfare with confidence. I will declare Your name, offering up praise to God. I will press into Your Word every day. I will scatter Your enemies through the power of Your blood.

LIFTING UP OTHERS

I believe in the power of Communion so much that I love to make confession over my family of how the blood of Jesus sets us free. This confession absolutely terrifies parts of darkness. I know from personal experience that it's the one thing of which they are absolutely terrified. They know that the blood of Jesus is the dividing line that separates someone the demonic can control from someone they can't touch.

I love to hold this before the Lord and pray for the people around me. I just plead the blood of Jesus over their lives. I want to encourage you to pick up a similar habit. It's not just grape juice that we're drinking. I pray that each of us would fully realize the effect of what we're doing during Communion. I believe that the Lord is going to release unusual miracles of healing in the taking of the bread. He is going to release unusual miracles of deliverance to people and family members who are maybe a thousand miles away or more by our taking the juice (representing the blood) and pleading the blood of Jesus over their lives.

Prayer while partaking of Communion is possibly one of the most underrated prayers that we could ever pray.

Communion is not a magic formula. It's us being convinced that the blood of Jesus sets free. And that expression of faith puts us into a position to influence the destinies of our families, the people around us, and the entire world.

Father, I want to lift up my loved ones today. I will speak out their names and plead the blood of Your Son, Jesus, over each and every one of them. Today, I will remind hell that it lost all authority on the earth. I release miraculous encounters with Heaven over each person I pray for, in the name of Jesus!

SAVED, HEALED, DELIVERED

The only requirement for you to take Communion is that you know Jesus Christ as your personal Savior. If that is not the case, you can confess your sins and invite Him to be the Lord of your life right now. There's no better moment than this one to step into His freedom and grace.

Jesus came as our example. Everything that Jesus did here on earth was an example for us to model in our daily lives. When Jesus speaks about the betrayal He will suffer, He turns around and praises God. God, help us to do the same.

Being rejected or betrayed has been a part of all of our lives. So just take a moment right now and ask yourself a few questions. Is there anyone you need to forgive? Is there anyone whom you have been unkind to? Ask God to forgive you, and commit to Him that you will go and make things right as soon as this is done.

If there is any bitterness or unforgiveness inside of you, you want to give that to Him. It's of no use to you; it will destroy you. Forgive anyone you need to forgive, and make it right with God right now.

Hold the bread in your hands.

This bread represents Jesus and His broken body. It represents our healing. Do you need healing in your body? Do you need emotional freedom? Is your spirit crushed and you need Jesus' healing touch? If you need a miracle, put your hand on your heart. We *are* healed. This is a prophetic depiction of all that Jesus would accomplish—peace, well-being, and healing.

You are healed.

Let's take the bread together.

Now, read this aloud with me:

And when He had taken a cup and given thanks, He gave it to them, saying, "Drink from it, all of you; for this is My blood of the [new and better] covenant, which [ratifies the agreement and] is being poured out for many [as a substitutionary atonement] for the forgiveness of sins" (Mathew 26:27-28 AMP).

Take the cup in your hands.

This cup represents the blood of Jesus, our salvation. Jesus' blood changed everything for each one of us. Forever. When that stone was rolled away, He rose in victory. We get to participate in that victory and live forever under the New Covenant. You and I are able to go boldly before the throne of Heaven. And we have a Savior who intercedes on our behalf. You will never be alone. You will never be found unworthy of His love.

By His blood, we have been saved. We are saved, healed, and delivered.

My body, my soul, and my spirit will be well in the name of Jesus. I will walk in total well-being. You died for me. Jesus, come. Thank You for Your broken body. Thank You for Your blood. I need Your healing presence, Jesus. Thank You that I can come to Your table freely and without shame. Thank You, Jesus, that You are here. Thank You that nothing stays the same in Your presence. Thank You that Your love for me is unending.

ABOUT BENI JOHNSON

Beni, along with her husband, Bill Johnson, was the senior pastor of Bethel Church. Beni had a call to intercession that remains an integral part of the Bethel Church mission. She was pivotal in the development of Bethel's Prayer House as well as the intercession team. Beni carried a call to see the church become healthy and whole in their bodies, souls, and spirits. Her passion for people, health, and intercession has all helped to bring the much-needed breakthrough in Bethel's ministry. Beni's vision was to see the people of God be filled with joyful prayer, intercession, and complete wellness.

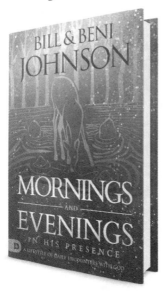

From
BENI JOHNSON

Miracles Wait at the Communion Table

For centuries, the Church has observed the Lord's Supper as part of corporate worship, instituted by Jesus Himself. But for many Christians today, this tradition can be a confusing ritual. Are we missing something in this ancient sacrament?

Beni and Bill Johnson—bestselling authors and senior leaders of Bethel Church in Redding, California—had a miraculous revelation while celebrating communion. In *The Power of Communion,* they reveal how this sacred practice is an often overlooked opportunity to release God's power in your life!

Don't settle for a lifeless routine. God is supernaturally present in the sacrament of Communion! Learn to embrace this prophetic act of remembrance, worship, warfare, and healing as it was always meant to be!

Purchase your copy wherever books are sold.

From
BENI JOHNSON

Intercession With Joy!

Beni Johnson's personal journey to becoming *The Happy Intercessor* takes you on an exciting adventure to capture the heartbeat of Heaven. From her violent shaking experience to the "thin place" between Heaven and earth where supernatural spirituality is commonplace, you will be amazed and empowered with the joy she shares.

Being addicted to God's presence brings comfort and peace to all believers—becoming a happy intercessor is within your reach. You can make a difference in your family, workplace, community, nation, and world.

You will be encouraged and inspired by the depth of love and knowledge shared in *The Happy Intercessor*. Even the weariest warrior will jump for joy as a cool, cleansing balm washes over your body, soul, and spirit.

Purchase your copy wherever books are sold.

We are a community of believers passionate
about God's manifest presence.

We believe that God is good and
our great privilege is to know and experience Him.

To learn more about church, music, events,
media, schools, and more, visit us at:

www.bethel.com

YOUR Prophetic
COMMUNITY

Are you passionate about hearing God's voice, walking with Jesus, and experiencing the power of the Holy Spirit?

Destiny Image is a community of believers with a passion for equipping and encouraging you to live the prophetic, supernatural life you were created for!

We offer a fresh helping of practical articles, dynamic podcasts, and powerful videos from respected, Spirit-empowered, Christian leaders to fuel the holy fire within you.

> **Sign up now to get awesome content delivered to your inbox**
> destinyimage.com/sign-up

 Destiny Image